I0769901

Copyright © Sandy Dacombe Ferrar.

All rights reserved. No part of this book may be used or reproduced in any manner whatsoever without written permission except in the case of brief quotations embodied in critical articles or reviews.

Cover design by S Ferrar
ISBN: 978 1979059626

Xafrica

Letters from the Southern Rift

Volume 1

Sandy Dacombe Ferrar

Introduction

Talking of Nature was one of the longest running programmes on the old SABC English Service radio station. It was discarded with the revamping of programmes when Radio South Africa became SAfm in 1995.

It began in the late sixties as a weekly panel-discussion, chaired by a young scientist with a very attractive speaking voice, Dr John Hanks, who was then with the infant Institute of Natural Resources in Natal. An ex-Zimbabwean, John had run a similar programme in Harare. One way or another, John has always been passionate about making the public aware of wildlife and its needs. He went on to be CEO of the South African Nature Foundation, which was linked to the World Wildlife Fund before South Africa became squeaky clean politically and the WWF could be seen to be involved without losing face. Then SANF just became the South African branch of WWF, and John moved on to running the trans-frontier reserves initiative, Peace Parks Foundation.

I came to the programme as I come to most things in my life—by annoying someone. When I joined the station, the ToN format had become a weekly half-hour magazine, circulating through the regions. Each region would suddenly realise on Thursday that the programme was their responsibility for the following day, and in the ensuing panic the interests of wildlife and conservation might just possibly be served, but not particularly memorably. I suggested that this was not doing the programme or the subject justice and found myself immediately elected producer/editor/presenter. Once I got over the terror, I loved it.

Possibly the most memorable thing about the programme, and the only aspect that never changed through a kaleidoscope of formats and presenters, was the signature tune. I have no idea who chose it, but the choice was brilliant. It was a charming, laid back bit of casual jazz composed by Cameroonian musician Manu Dibango, called "Wild Man in the City". Behind the haunting, woody sounds of sax, flute and guitar was a hint of water and distant ducks. I'm told it's commercially available, and I keep looking for it, which has led to my investing in one or two other Manu Digbango CD's, but I've not found it.

Talking of Nature gave me an excuse to get out into the bush, and it gave me licence to ask. Before, I felt nervous about bothering those intellectual giants, the wildlife scientists, with my puny little numb-skull questions. But once I was asking on the behalf of the general public I knew that it may be a stupid question, but someone out there was bound to want to know. It was wonderfully freeing. And the cherry on the top, the thing that really made it precious to me, was that I could experience everything twice—once in the actual experience, and again as I mentally and verbally re-created it for the listeners. Mae West was right about too much of a good thing, it *is* wonderful.

It's been a while since I was Talking of Nature, but the seasons keep rolling round. Today it's officially Spring. The first ragged garlands of swallows have graced the china-blue sky and the black collared barbets are re-affirming their vows on the edge of my feeding table. Somewhere out of sight a black sunbird is whistling his sweet cascade of notes, and jasmine sends tendrils of erotic perfume into farther corners of the garden to seduce the bees.

There is so much still to talk about. And since radio and I agreed amicably to go our separate ways, I have formed a new relationship with the cyclops on my desk. Instead of sharing my thoughts through a microphone, I'll be chatting to you through the one-eyed monster that links your desk to mine. Since I won't have to speak out loud, these chats are going to be a lot less formal, more relaxed and intimate—I'll sometimes even give you a glimpse of the scientists through my eyes, and not just what he or she thinks. I look forward to sharing all the delights, surprises and bewilderment of this complex and beautiful world we inhabit, and the fascinating people who study it.

Why X-Africa?

It began through a conversation with a young safari guide. He was tall, broad shouldered, tanned skin nicely crinkly around his blue eyes. He was not exactly coming on to me, but he was making it subtly clear that this was an option if I wished. I know I'm relatively attractive, but I'm not exactly a femme fatal, and I found his attitude a little surprising. So l asked him about it.

The dear lad saw this as part of his responsibilities as a safari operator. Taking care of the client's every need. I'm pretty sure this was not entirely a matter of selfless dedication to duty. Judging by his complacency, he probably got a fair amount of job satisfaction from this aspect—more than, say, from repairing game fences, anyway. Far from being charmed by the idea, I found it all a little too coldly calculating. But it did make me think.

The fact is that the African bush is, for a woman, almost unbearably romantic.

Sometime later I found myself submerged in this phenomenon yet again. The bush-wise, leather-skinned, beaten-up research scientist at my elbow, who just then was looking irresistibly attractive, listened to my story about the safari guide with interest.

"He's right," he said. "The bush is sexy. It's a known thing. Why do you think safaris are so popular? Because it makes people all squeaky between the legs."

Now this is one of the fundamental differences between men and women. Blatant is not a turn-on for most women. Subtle, yes; direct—very seldom. Unaware that he had probably blown his chances, he finished by saying, "If you can put the essence of Africa into words, it will sell like..." and he used a simile involving dubious confectionaries in a religious establishment.

That shut me down completely. Interesting that some men can't see the difference between titillating and plain offensive. Personal disappointment aside, these rather obnoxious men are right. They've accepted with uncomplicated pleasure that this is so, but it's more difficult for a woman to accept, so I've been worrying at it for years.

I think it's to do with vulnerability. For a woman anyway. Being out there—away from temperature regulating equipment and protection from the elements like roofs, and glass windows and carpets— when you get the feel of the breeze on your skin, the sun on your neck and the touch of grass on your legs, and there is nothing between you and the far blue hills but open space and quiet air, you start to recapture a little of what it means to be alive, human, and unarmed in a space that is not designed specifically for your personal survival. Suddenly all your senses are out on stalks, and it's a wonderfully exhilarating feeling. It feels daring. You feel very small and fragile, and men suddenly look rather big and re-assuring. And all that adds up to sexy.

Then came a little chat with the web-master of wildnetafrica.com, Dr Andrew McKenzie, himself once a wild-life vet. Andrew kindly provided me with space on his web and what today would be called a blog—and in exchange I wrote a story, and later a letter, every two weeks, which his staff posted up for me. It was a wonderful way for me to continue doing what I had loved most about radio. Ideally I hoped to find a sponsor who would provide me with the wherewithal to make this a permanent occupation.

Andrew smiled at my dream, and gently pointed out that the one thing that really sells well on the web is sex, and the challenge was clear. As the scientist phrased it, "Put the essence of Africa into words."

So I began to spell Africa with an X.

January, February & March 1999

Blatant baboons
18th January

Last week a friend and I took our sketching equipment and wandered through the Pretoria zoo—or the National Zoological Gardens, to give the correct title.

The wonderful thing about sketching materials is that they give you an excuse to sit very still and gaze at whatever happens to be before your eyes, and not actually do anything. This is rare today. Today if you sit quietly for more than two minutes a dark voice in the back of your skull will begin a low rumbling that sounds very like Industry rebuking Idleness. However, if you have a pen or a crayon in your hand, the moment the first hint of that sound begins, you can banish it with a few random swipes at the paper. And if you do this long enough, you might even start to see some likeness in the random swipes to whatever it is you are looking at.

The most impressive thing that happens when you sit in one place very quietly is that your mind gets bored and wanders off. It's amazing what it finds to play with. Take the Hamadryas baboons for instance.

Ethiopian in origin, they seem a little smaller than our southern chacma baboon, but the females share the characteristic of hugely distended bottoms when in season. In the Hamadryas, the swelling is a rich red. The pick of the males goes to the female with the biggest and brightest bottom. To anything other than a male baboon, this is astoundingly unattractive. In fact, it looks painful. Zoo staff report being inundated with complaints from irate visitors that the baboons are suffering from terrible infections and the animals deserve to be better cared for.

Idly eyeing these rosy invitations to procreate the species my friend remarked, "Thank God for small mercies. Imagine having to wear huge baggy trousers to work to hide that lot."

The facts of the matter are sobering. Female baboons are demure in comparison to humans. At least they only hang out the flags when the festival is on, so to speak. Take a long quiet look at female Homo supposedly-sapiens. We must be the only mammal to wander round with hugely distended mammary glands. All the time. Other mammals only do that when they are actually nursing young. We start inflating them as we enter the breeding arena, and most of the time we don't even bother to deflate them after we stop being fertile. Let's not plead ignorance here. We are, all of us, deeply aware that they are a sexual trigger, and designed to provoke procreation. Do we wear big baggy tops to work to keep from distracting the males? Not a chance.

And yet those of us who regard ourselves as being enlightened, emancipated and empowered are hugely annoyed at being judged as potential mates by the size of our nursery equipment. Ironic, isn't it?

The Ecological case against Vets
1st February

One of the fascinating side lights in matters of life and death in the wild is the attitude of ecologists toward veterinary surgeons.

I was discussing the subject of management strategy within the Kruger National Park with consulting ecologist Tony Ferrar (ex CEO of the South African Wildlife Society), a man known to call a spade by its common or garden name. He pointed out that for years Kruger management has been subject to the criticism that it reacts to symptoms, rather than researching causes. That it makes ecological management decisions from a veterinary perspective. Vets, says Tony, regard a sick animal as a failure. They are trained to focus on individual animals. Ecologists are concerned with populations and communities. Where a vet sees a sick animal as a call to action, to the ecologist that same animal is a vital food source for other animals. To an ecologist, getting rid of sickness is bad policy. The scientific thing to do, says Ferrar, is to research the causes and monitor the symptoms of the disease.

"Management decisions should be based on research, not on beating symptoms to death."
What fascinated me was the implication that vets are not scientists. Worse still, that vets have a mind-set that is anti-ecological.

And blow me down if Prof Rudi van Aarde of the Mammal Research Institute didn't say exactly that. When I asked why it was that the two teams of vets on the elephant family-planning merry-go-round drew such a blank, his immediate reply was, "Vets are not scientists," and echoed what Ferrar had said, adding that vets are highly qualified technicians, but they make appalling ecologists.

Management decisions influenced by vets resulted in the wholesale extermination of game in an attempt to control trypanosomiasis in Rhodesia. In 1958 alone 14 911 animals were shot as part of the

Tsetse Control Hunting Programme. The tsetse fly are still there.

Also in the 50s, buffalo were fingered as carriers of foot and mouth disease, and there were insistent calls for the elimination of the entire buffalo population. "Destruction of Buffalo Orders" were promulgated in some countries. Luckily the storm of protest from those much maligned conservationists, the hunters, resulted in herds of so-called "disease-free" buffalo being built up, and these have been reintroduced in areas where "disease control" eliminated the species. The destruction goes on, but the vets have still to prove how the disease moves from buffalo to cattle.

And that's another interesting point. You will notice that these measures are taken not for the good of wildlife, but for the protection of domestic cattle. The entire ethical foundation for vets seems to depend on the survival of domestic livestock.

Vets have always been among my favourite people. I'm not at all sure how I feel about this.

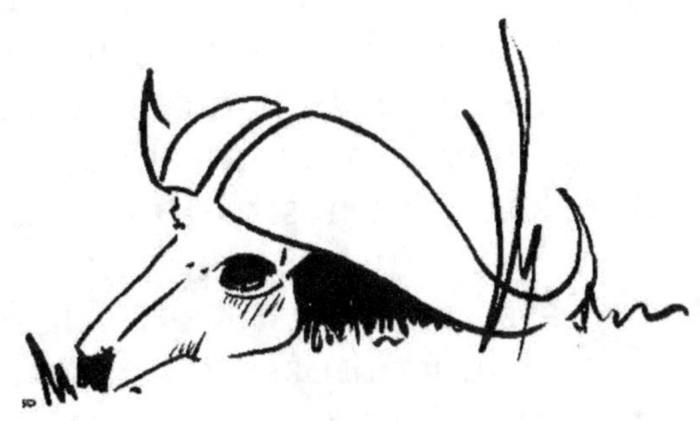

Rita's weekend
8ᵗʰ February

I have somehow accumulated a handful of wildly special friends. Take Rita, for example. Rita is the kind of person who will suddenly phone at seven on a Friday morning to tell me she is picking me up at eight for a weekend in the Kruger National Park.

When she did, I felt like a cross between a skiving school kid and a stunned mullet, but obediently I threw stuff into a bag, and by the time we'd got to Belfast, Rita had tracked down the only vacant hut in the entire park. I have to admit there are times that a cell phone justifies its existence.

Perhaps the hut was vacant because it was number 13. Rita was born on the 13th and her life has not been all bad, so that didn't bother us. The hut overlooked the not-so-distant staff accommodation and that may also have had something to do with its availability. But, knowing it's virtually impossible to get into the park without booking anything from six months to two years in advance, we shrugged and were grateful. The feeling encompassed the entire weekend. With the full moon glaring down we sat at three in the morning watching a huge bull elephant just four metres away—on the other side of the fence—

delicately stripping the new shoots off an utterly battered tree. He had been so silent and made such minutely rustling sounds I was sure he was a mouse at our corn-flakes. Rita was the one who got up to see, and came and called me.

We saw just about everything except leopard, but we saw the remains of a leopard kill—a gutted impala wedged in the fork of a tree. The place was thick with buffalo, elephants, lions, even rhino. The veld itself looked very sad and chomped to the nub, but the dombeyas were in full bloom, and the sweet-thorn had started hanging out its scented catkins and absolutely everything had babies—zebra, waterbuck, giraffe, warthog—and nothing looking stressed after a long dry winter.

The birds were a delight. A secretary bird stood fluffing out its feathers in the golden light on our first game drive. At least we could identify that one, and bateleur and cape vulture, but we saw an embarrassing number of raptors that left us feeling confused and silly. Soon we gave up and allowed ourselves just to gawp at the power and grace and the swift sweep of wings.

A black-headed oriole sat in the fig tree outside our hut on Saturday afternoon and called insistently till we walked out to admire him. Then he flaunted his mate at us and flew away. The next morning a green pigeon swanked around in the same tree, showing off her yellow pantaloons. We saw secretary birds again, and ground hornbills glimpsed through the leafless scrub.

Like a dream sequence from some romantic movie, a magnificent pair of lions materialised in the lion-coloured grass and mated with an intensity and focus that made us feel invisible. Robert Redford and Meryl Streep seemed positively insipid by comparison. We drove back to camp with the full moon rising in the windscreen, and the setting sun blazing an African red in the rear-view mirror. A herd of wildebeest drifted like smoke between grey trees.

Sunday was softly overcast giving the whole day a pearlescent glow. A weekend to treasure. Not to mention the friend.

When the culls stopped
22nd February

For years the Kruger National Park was at loggerheads with the rest of the world regarding their elephant management strategy. Well, that's not quite true, since the strategy was in place and operating for quite a while before the world found out about it and decided that it was unacceptable.

The theory was that if you confine elephants to one area, they will simply keep on breeding and eating everything in sight until you have a dustbowl full of elephant carcasses. Peter Beard wrote a blackly beautiful, despairing book on the subject of just such an occurrence at Tsavo (Starvo) National Park in Kenya, called *The End of the Game*. So, since elephants tend to be very hard on their environment—stripping off branches and bark and pulling up roots while feeding, pushing trees over as a test of strength or just to while away a few idle hours—logic would seem to indicate that the fewer elephants you have, the better it is for the bush.

Back in 1903 the Kruger had about thirty elephants. By 1967 they had six and a half thousand.

Next comes the question: What do you do with too many elephants? Well, back in the bad old days, that wasn't seen as a problem. You used them in the same way as mankind uses any abundant resource. There's an awful lot of steak on one elephant. The hide makes good leather. The tusks have been prized alongside gold and jewels since time began. Even the tail hairs have been used as bracelets by early hunters and modern game-rangers. An abundance of these resources is not a disadvantage. In fact, a dead elephant has a higher market value than a live one.

And so the culls began. Prof. Rudi van Aarde of the University of Pretoria's Mammal Research Institute tells me that between 1967 and when the culls stopped in 1995 seventeen thousand elephants were killed.

But what was useful to the scientists, Rudi tells me, is that in 1984 the Park got a little wiser and divided the area into quarters. From an annual aerial census they would assess the number of elephant above the "ideal", estimated by what Rudi calls 'abdominal biology', another name for gut feeling. Then they would go out and cull that number from just one quarter of the Park, where previously they had traumatised the entire population by culling throughout. Apart from giving three quarters of the Park's elephants a less stressful life, it also meant that Rudi and his team could begin to assess the response of the group to the removal.

The findings were startling. In effect the cull would create a sort of vacuum, which we know nature abhors. And elephants would stream in to fill it. So trying to save the environment by lessening elephant numbers actually had the result of increasing pressure on the environment for the next year as the elephant population more than doubled its number in that area. Far from stabilising the number of elephants, the culls were proving that the lower the elephant density, the higher the population growth rate became.

And you thought they stopped culling because of public outcry.

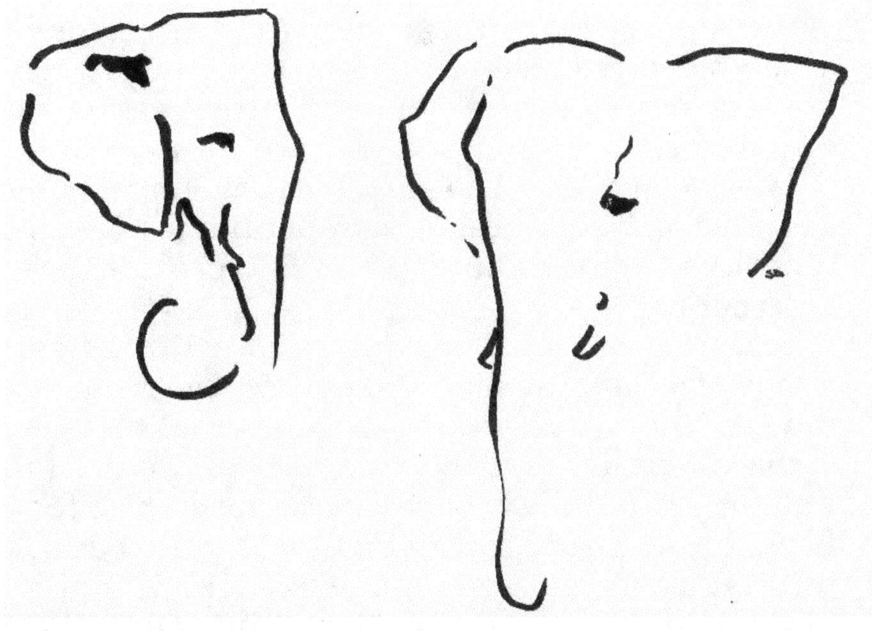

Swartkrans[1]
1ˢᵗ March

On the last Friday in winter Dr Francis Thackeray drove me to see the place where man first tamed fire. That was not the main aim and goal of the drive. I had not seen any of the sites that form the treasure-house of our early beginnings, and since he was going out there that day, and I had agreed to help him adjudicate an environmental essay competition, we sensibly came up with the solution that would provide the most entertainment.

Sterkfontein, Swartkrans and Kromdraai lie almost within walking distance of each other. But though the three sites exist in time together as archaeological digs, they were not always so. In three million years, quite a lot changes. The climate for one. Back then, these grassy high-veld hills were sub-tropical woodland, perhaps even forest, moist and hung with vines. Our ancestors who found the first cave had not yet discarded the opposed big-toe, so

---

[1] An early glimpse of what later became the Cradle of Mankind World Heritage Site where Lee Burger stunned the world with the discovery of *Homo naledi*.

useful for climbing, in favour of the long sleek foot for speed over open veld.

But even that changed over another million years. Cometh the veld, cometh the foot. The brain got bigger and the teeth and jaw got smaller, so tools got more important—also as protection now that the soft underbelly was right in the line of attack from any charging creature. But they were still little folk, these tool makers or users, with a skull that fits comfortably into one of my not-so-large hands. These were the fire-tamers, the first slow blossoming of what Hawthorn called "the black flower of civilisation".

Gazing down into the romantic and evocative terraces of the Swartkrans dig is a sobering feeling. Francis beside me bubbled with excitement at seeing the half-moon, milky in the almost spring afternoon  sky, hung poetically above the hump of the protective hill, like a beacon above the plunging depth to mankind's first hearth. It took a while for me to see the link that was so obvious to Francis—man's first experiment with flame which ultimately lead to the first tentative step in space travel, the moon landing. From toasting your meat to strapping a giant flame to your backside. Big thrill.

For Francis, ever the joyous optimist, humanity is the most wonderful creature on earth. I, on the other hand, find it hard to shake off the knowledge of war in the Congo, bombs at American embassies, genocide in Rwanda, border disputes in the Middle East. Man's playing with fire invented the AK 47, the atom bomb and that greatest of all killers, the motor car. Man's inhumanity seems uppermost. Emanating from the fern-hung depths of Swartkrans, where the plaintive falling note of the red-winged starling sounds like a lament, is an almost damp brooding which feels to me like a sense of insidious evil.

Interesting, isn't it? I really do like people. Like Francis, for instance—his fizzing energy and glorious enthusiasm. And it was a most entertaining afternoon, I thoroughly enjoyed myself. I just don't think very highly of mankind. Cars too. I can go quite gaga over a particular model, but the cancerous mass of traffic and the slowly tightening web of highways and through-routes and trans-continental corridors seems likely to trap and strangle the earth.

Yes, it's been a giant leap—but where are we in relation to the frying-pan?

Kafue National Park
Zambi, 8th March

Kafue is the second largest National Park in Africa. Like the rest of Zambia, Kafue has had a tough time. The country had nothing much other than wildlife and copper, and when the bottom dropped out of the copper market, the wildlife got eaten. Not all of it, of course. A huge portion of Zambia (some 30%) is declared a conservation area of some sort or another, but policing that amount of land without adequate resources is a hopelessly impossible task.

Poaching aside, there is nothing quite like a bit of neglect to make a wilderness area worth discovering. You've got to be fairly determined, though, since part of the road from Lusaka is recognised as the worst in Zambia and it compares pretty evenly with the worst I saw in Mozambique a few years back. There are one or two privately run camps, but the most charming place I saw was Kafwala, owned and operated by the Zambian Wildlife Society. It is self-catering and very small, overlooking palm-fringed rapids in the river.

Kafue is such a huge area that I only saw the northern section, and not much of that in two brief days. But in that time I was delighted to meet the Defassa waterbuck which was new to me, and see a herd of twenty or so roan antelope, which I'd not seen in the flesh before. I had not realised how big they are—almost as tall as eland—nor how silly those tufted ears look. Also new to me was Lichtenstein's hartebeest, looking very striking with black muzzles and black uneven patches on the flanks, seasonal markings acquired by nosing around in the burned stubble for fresh shoots.

Another first for me, making four in less than an hour, was puku, a fuzzy high-bottomed buck with a heart-shaped nose, looking like a russet-coloured cross between impala and waterbuck.

Zambia is a country blessed with rivers, and a large portion of the populace is dependent on fish. The Kafue River itself, for all its impressive size, seems almost overburdened with dependants and the stretch that I saw had tall fish weirs straddling the tributaries, each a huge mesh of young trees stripped from the fringing forest. In the old days, I'm told, one would need to get permission from the local chief to cut down a tree, and the request would have to be well justified to be granted. The fish weirs make prolific use of young growth. Despite the fact that it's hard to see how the narrow strip of riverine forest can support these ubiquitous structures, and how the river can continue to supply enough fish, the weirs themselves are amazingly beautiful. To me they seem like the fossilised spines of huge extinct creatures—strong and graceful bones. I spent a bewitched hour picnicking downstream of one, watching a wealth of water birds feasting there— African finfoot, giant kingfisher, greenbacked heron, jacana.

If you plan to go, make sure you have a well-equipped 4x4 and expect only whatever you take with you. Remember also that Kafue National Park lies across the main road between the Zambian capital Lusaka and Angola, and any tension in the latter will reflect in the attitude of the Zambian security forces who guard the bridge across the Kafue River.

Marabou Stork
18th March

He stood with his back to us,
looking indigent and depressed, as they always do. His bald head was pulled down into his hunched shoulders, and his thin legs looked pale and blotchy.

It's those legs particularly that are the focus of this little tale, though the entire marabou is something of a puzzle. For a start that rather embarrassing pouch that dangles from its throat—it's too far up the body to be what it really looks like, and both male and female marabous are equipped with it, and anyway, birds don't have them. Not any that look like they've been borrowed from an elderly white hunter, anyway. That pouch is an air sac, I'm told, and is inflated possibly for heat dispersal, but certainly for display—either a sign of dominance or a territorial warning. Apparently there is another at the back of the neck that looks like a lump of steak when it's inflated, just what one would wish to have at the back of one's neck. And of course the bird is bald because it's a carrion eater, like the vultures, and a feathered head is a nuisance when your living is made by picking the moist insides out of aromatic carcasses.

But the legs! The legs! Since these storks look very like dissolute Dickensian undertakers—bald headed and clean shaven, with snowy neck-cloths and a shabby black tail-coats—the legs look like they are decked out in rather scruffy white spats. The fact of the matter is that the marabou has black legs. The white is carefully applied by the stork him/herself, through deliberate directing of the cloaca (arsehole to us unscientific types). Again, no-one seems terribly sure why this is done, since most birds are careful to aim the other way. The general thought is that it's a method of cooling down, and with the African sun beating down on your bald head, I suppose one might, in desperation . . . actually, no, I can't see it. Nevertheless, that's what they do, with an interesting white-washed look as the result.

This is where the tale really begins. My scientific advisor was pointing out this interesting habit to me. Clearly enjoying my admiration for his boundless knowledge he proceeded to explain that the REAL reason for the application of this self-prepared white-wash is because the storks stand still for so long. There was a pause while I thought about that.

He glanced sideways at my puzzled face and said, "It's a termite repellent."

The system, he explained, was so successful that it was soon adopted by Africa's early colonialists, who, in imitation of the marabou's termite management plan, white-washed the bases of all the trees lining their roads, since trees also have a habit of standing still for quite a long time. On one leg. The tree-bole-white-wash tradition is still maintained in some areas, as he pointed out to me as we drove through Livingstone. Irrefutable evidence of the truth of his theory.

And quite honestly, if it comes to a personal choice, I'll settle for the termite-control explanation over heat-defeatment any day. Admittedly because it makes me laugh and it's a glorious story, especially coming from a dedicated scientist.

For the more level-headed of us, the habit is called uro-hydration, and it's not just the marabou that does it. The migrant Adbim's stork does it too, and so do several others. But it really would be nice to know exactly why—and I'd like to know about the marabou's air sacs too.

By the way, the name marabout in Arabic means hermit or holy-man. Marabou without the "t" is a trade name for the feathers—taken from the under-tail coverts—which are used for trimming hats. A bit of fashion-conscious arse-about-face.

Funny Malarious
29ᵗʰ March

Truly it's no laughing matter. Malaria is rampant in Africa, and some strains of it are deadly. But there is no escaping the fact that it's funny peculiar. For a start there is the fallacy that the warning symptoms of malaria are like 'flu. "If you start feeling like you've got 'flu two weeks after you've been in an infested area, go and get a blood test," the know-alls will tell you.

What they don't tell you is that it can take a lot longer than two weeks for the symptoms to show. So don't feel safe if you haven't had a runny nose or a sore throat within two weeks. Also, it doesn't feel like 'flu. Or at least it didn't for me; for me it was like a cross between a spontaneous hangover and the onset of a vicious pregnancy.

I'd been run-down and a bit off-colour (like my jokes) for a few days, but out of the blue came a crashing headache that seemed to cram my head down onto my chest, while my stomach went into revolt and was planning to jettison its entire contents via the most available exit. Naturally it wasn't interested in informing me which exit that would be. Since I happened to be in church at the time this was a trifle awkward. Avoiding a spew in the pew called for fast action, and my head was telling me it had lost the operating manual for my feet and legs. The entire evacuation (of me from the church, not of my stomach—let us retain some semblance of decorum) was conducted by what felt like remote control, but I made it home and crawled miserably into bed. Despite enthusiastic encouragement from friends to seek medical advice, all I cared about was lying still.

That's the catch. And I suspect it's what makes malaria a killer. It's just impossible to lever your carcass out of bed, or to even to think of doing that, let alone going to the trouble of phoning a medic, or planning transport or whatever. And if you're a bit of a loner, you've got a real problem. For most of us the family gets very alarmed and rallies round and causes things to get done with or without our own active participation. And once the bugs in your blood have been identified and the treatment begins, it's usually a short—if unpleasant—route to recovery.

It's a dreadful disease. You don't feel like moving, and then you find you can't. You're too weak to get up and pee on your own, and one minute your veins are full of iced water and you're colder than the north face of Everest and the next you're sweating from the unbearable heat. Just the movement of air across your arm makes every little hair follicle ache. Believe me, it's not fun. If you catch it in time, you recover. If not, probably not. So I dread to think what it could have been like if I had been on my own, convinced that whatever I was suffering from couldn't be malaria, as it was more than two weeks since I was exposed and it didn't feel like 'flu.

Don't take chances. Don't think it's kinda smart or double-rugged to have been to Africa and weathered the disease—been there, done that, got the night-sweats. Don't risk it. It's a killer. Get expert medical advice before you come here, and do as you're told. Africa has enough sad statistics, you don't need to become another.

April, May & June

Hello, David Shepherd
Zambia, 6th April

My scientific adviser and I were trundling down towards the old slave post of Feira—now called Luangwa—on a dimly overcast day at the start of the rainy season. The green box-shaped land rover was looking very business-like; the driver, my companion and scientific adviser was looking his usual blend of the bush-battered and the scientifically suave. But not the least artistic. The object was to explore a little of the lower Luangwa valley, and see the old town of Feira at the confluence of the Luangwa and the Zambezi, the point where three countries meet.

On our way in toward the little town, we found the police barrier down—a boom lowered across the dirt-road next to a dusty cluster of official huts. The police officer came hurrying out to us, relieved to find a vehicle that could give his detective a lift to town. A miscreant had broken out of jail the night before, and was headed for Feira and freedom. Our help was needed in getting the nervous detective into town sooner than the evil-doer might expect. As the officer approached our car, his expression of business-like concern changed miraculously into one of great joy and delight. He raced up to the window, and gazed at Tony with pride and wonder.

"Oh," he cried, "It is you! Welcome, Mr Shepherd!" We laughed out loud, amused at his mistake and touched by his pleasure. Tony did a regal David Shepherd impression, smiling benignly and shaking hands warmly, but chose not to tarnish the moment with the truth, and we drove away smiling.

Here the river banks are quite densely populated and have been for centuries, since the annual floods bring a rich alluvial top-dressing—good for a quick crop or two. Then trees were chopped out to create more lands, and the floods just sweep the ground away. Gradually the area has become eroded, over-grazed and arid looking. Clumps of palms and palm scrub survive, and the occasional baobab and stately winter thorn or apple ring acacia. Between these, little villages nestle, looking neat and clean. Of course the buffalo thorn, our *'wag'n-bietjie'* is nurtured, since a local alcoholic beverage called *'katchaso'* is brewed from the berries. Flowering shrubs like the white bauhinia and the enigmatic 'fried-egg' bush give a mist of bridal white, and butterflies abound. It's an area of long established subsistence farming, but not without charm for all of that.

Perched on a hill above the confluence, the only new thing in the little town of Feira is its change of name; it is as well-worn and tired as the rest of the countryside. It obviously makes its living in the old way—no, not slave trading, the other old way, fishing. The scent of drying fish permeates the little hill-top settlement, with fish hung to dry from whatever surface comes to hand—washing-lines, roof-eaves, fences. Beyond, the two rivers merge each emptying from a narrow deep channel and smoothing away as one. The northern banks of both rivers, Mozambique across the way here, and Zambia herself seen from the Zambezi, are heavily populated. In contrast the Zimbabwean shore looks excitingly wild and mysterious, deep green with riverine vegetation and the rich forested look that would have been on this side too, before the fishermen and farmers settled. The area is Kanyemba, and tucked away into the trees are a few lucrative fishing-safari camps.

On the spit of land where the two big rivers merge, fishermen and traders work together at packing dried fish into drum-shaped parcels of palm-fibre and bark—each little fish an opulently scented dark butterfly—carefully packed, heads outward, tails in, neat concentric circles of dried protein headed for the city of Lusaka.

The Real David Shepherd

British born conservationist David Shepherd, CBE is one of those remarkable men who has managed to make a living out of what he loves doing. On top of that he has managed to make a lot of money for what he loves, too.

An artist specialising in military and aviation subjects, he was sent to Kenya by the RAF and lost his heart to Africa and her wildlife. Subsequently he devoted himself to exploring on canvas the essence that moved him so. Through the sale of his work and public appearances he has contributed significantly to wildlife conservation, and Zambia in particular, a favourite haunt, has been a recipient of his generosity. So it's not surprising that he is well-known even (or perhaps one should say "especially") in the more remote areas of the country. David is recognised as one of the world's leading wildlife artists.

My scribble is taken from a photographic portrait of David working in the bush, calmly sketching a "jumbo" from life. If you look carefully, you will recognise immediately his staggering likeness to Tony Ferrar, little known wildlife ecologist, entertaining bush-illuminator and unwitting David Shepherd impersonator.

Pilanesberg National Park
South Africa, 28th April

Since I wrote this, much has changed. I have not visited Pilanesberg since this piece was written, and I'm told that the park has suffered terribly from neglect. This makes me very sad, but pleased that I have written something of what Pilanesberg was when the park was young and beautiful.

The only thing that is cumbersome about Pilanesberg is its name. But once you've grasped that it's named after Chief Pilane of the Bafokeng people who own the land, it stops being a nuisance. And it is a Berg too. Sort of.

It's actually the relic of a circular cluster of volcanic upheavals several million years ago. My scientific advisor tells me it's like a carbuncle rather than a single volcano, which would have erupted like a boil. Eeeu. If you have a medical frame of reference I hope you will be more amused by the simile than us less hardened common folk. Actually, right now there is nothing less like a suppuration than the Pilanesberg. The sheltering ring of hills creates a perfect natural stronghold for wildlife, and the barrier of high ground protects the visitor from the harsh reality of urban sprawl outside.

Less than two hours by car from Johannesburg, Pilanesberg is about double the size of Kenya's Ngorongoro crater. I can tell you no more about the differences, not having seen the latter, but I can tell you that Pilanesberg is a wonder on three separate counts. Firstly because it is such a perfect microcosm of the wider African landscape, a kind of "potted Africa", with plains and hills and bush and water and arid regions, and the exhilarating sense of space and freedom.

The second wonder is that being such a complex environment it provides natural habitats for animals almost never seen together—like the impala, our most common antelope, and the springbok, southern Africa's only gazelle and found in the more arid savannah plains. The same goes for the two more spectacular species of antelope, the arid open country gemsbok (fawn-grey, black and white with stunning straight horns rising upright from the head; real designer-antelope) and the even larger sable (in conventional black with white accessories and elegantly back-swept horns, arching over subtle russet-backed ears) which is more water dependent and found in open woodland areas. The area also has both the square-lipped "white" rhino, who behaves much like a single-minded lawn-mower, and the "black" rhino, more bad-tempered and unpredictable, with a little pointy prehensile lip for stripping leaves off shrubbery. The first likes open plains, the second lurks in thick bush. But you might see both in one day in Pilanesberg.

The third wonder is likely not to be seen at all by the casual visitor—which is what makes it such a wonder. It's the now historic transformation of Pilanesberg from a long settled, mainly farming area to apparent pristine wilderness. Dead-straight regional trunk roads have been subtly curved and the old scars re-vegetated; mine adits are over-grown with indigenous bush, but can be explored on guided walking trails; ploughed and cleared lands are now a sea of shimmering veld grasses, and barren over-grazed and eroded soil has been coaxed back to life and stability. The discerning eye can still spot a slightly unnatural tree-line here and there that speaks of agriculture, and the tourist-centre is the original Magistrate's Court revamped to a new purpose. Other than that, there is almost no trace of the rather negligent stewardship of the past. Not long past either, just twenty years. Pilanesberg is a text-book example of brilliant applied restoration ecology.

More importantly, if you're a bird-watcher, it's absolute heaven. Sitting quietly under the trees at the Education Centre we saw crimson-breasted shrike, paradise fly-catcher, ground-scraper thrush, and the rare pied babbler without having to move our heads more than 45 degrees. The little grove of thorn trees was alive with feathered fauna.

Pilanesberg has a variety of accommodation options, from luxury lodges to private tented camps to a caravan park. Its proximity to Sun City and its fabulous spawn the Lost City make it a bit of a Cinderella as far as big-bucks earning is concerned, but it is certainly not down-at-heel or unkempt at all. It's probably one of the best maintained and managed parks in South Africa[2], and its visitor ratings are skyrocketing.

Late winter is the best time for game-viewing (that's August, September) but if you just want to enjoy the beauty of the bush, the first flush of growth after the rains in November and December is the most magical. As summer progresses the vegetation gets lusher and thicker, so spotting game can be more of a challenge. If you're a bird specialist, summer is the time when the interesting migrant visitors are in the park, and bird behaviour is most interesting to watch.

Of course, if you're lucky enough to live within reach of the park you can experience all of Pilanesberg's facets over a series of weekend or day visits.

---

[2] Now one of the most devastatingly neglected

Matobo Hills, Zimbabwe
19th April

Just a reminder that this was written seventeen years ago; the Matobo Hills may not have changed much, but Zimbabwe's situation has worsened considerably. Spare a thought for all in this beautiful country who are going through desperate times.

There are certain places on the earth's crust that just have something extra. If you are one of the few who can feel ley-lines, you have a built-in explanation. Others believe that it's a matter of energy getting an added zing through granite particles, like light through a prism. Some say it's the presence of the ancestors that provide the frisson. I really don't know. But I do know that there are places that have been sacred from time immemorial, and they still feel special today. Like the Matobo Hills.

Perhaps it's a very simple thing that seems to have been known to the architects of all the great cathedrals—if you can get the eye to sweep upward, the spirit will follow. And the spirit soars among these huge tumbled boulders and rising whalebacks. Not that they're all that high, you understand, just that they are so... utterly... oh-wow-ish.

But together with the other-worldly awe that this landscape invokes, there is a very here-and-now satisfaction about the place. It's like a superbly well thought out Japanese garden. These perfectly balanced and poised boulders are in counterpoint to lush vegetation from the run-off in the wet, and the result is a symphony of textures. Between up-thrust heaps of boulders, each like a giant fossilised mole-hill, are serene plains of spear-grass rippling in the breeze, and a dense deep green of thick bush clusters at the base of each outcrop to thread its way towards the top. Paperbark albizia (*Albizia tanganyicensis*) and the mountain syringa (*Kirkia acuminata*), their bark satin and matt, throw dappled shade over the rocks and Zimbabwe aloes (*Aloe excelsa*) fierce and proud as tribal warriors stand sentry duty between them. Here and there a single dramatic euphorbia forms an exclamation point against the skyline, and the clouds seem to compete in the elegance stakes with the snaggle-toothed, exuberant geology.

This is the perfect habitat for dassies—fuzzy little tailless, round-eared rock-rabbits, who somehow always manage to look like bad museum specimens. The wildlife web here is mainly a dassie-driven economy, and their abundance ensures the presence of leopards and eagles. The black (*Verreaux's*) eagle in particular thrives, and nests here in densities considerably higher than any other large raptor anywhere in the world.

Less spectacular and more confiding are the stubby little klipspringers who teeter through the boulders like squat little quadruped ballet dancers. These tiny antelope are unique in that their fur is composed of something more like springy hollow quills than single strands of hair. These provide an insulating layer in extremes of heat and cold, and made the fur a popular stuffing for saddles back in the bad old days when off-road riding was the norm since there were no roads anyway. It's been suggested that this coat forms extra protection for the little buck if they should slip on the rocks, but a klipspringer losing its footing is about as common as a bird missing the perch, so it's a nice idea but hard to swallow.

If you are going to Zimbabwe, allow a day at the very minimum to experience the Matobo Hills. But be warned. It is a National Park, and Zimbabwe knows its value. Take PLENTY of money. It costs to get in at the gate, and there is an extra fee to visit Rhodes' grave at World's View. And if you pay the guide at the view-site, he will feed the lizards for you. There is also a charge for picnicking, and another for camping. Every time you look around, you'll find yet another official homing in for another charge. There is also a fenced-off wildlife park, and of course there is a separate entrance fee there too.

We were not the only visitors to be taken aback by the cost, a group of German tourists were bitterly disappointed at not having enough money with them to enter the park. There is also some complication about whether you pay in Zim dollars or US dollars— something about having to have exactly the right amount in the latter, since they cannot give change, and are not allowed to change the latter for the former. So go well stocked with both, and take plenty film for your camera, or your water-colour paints. It's worth it.

Problems in Paradise
5th May

Recreating paradise, a task set twenty years ago[3] for Pilanesberg National Park management, has not been uncomplicated. Returning the ground to its original condition—or as close as humanly possible—was the more easily managed part. Restocking the area with the quantity and variety of wildlife that would originally have been found there was fraught with difficulties.

Take for instance the problem of elephants. Having been banished for over a century by the farming community, these huge creatures are vital to the smooth running of a natural ecosystem. As a cross between a bulldozer and a mobile compost heap, an elephant plays a role in preventing bush-encroachment and redistributing the nutrients supplied by plants. There are certain seeds that cannot germinate unless they have passed through the acid bath of an elephants gut.

---

[3] At time of writing

The main difficulty in translocating elephants is that they are very big. So Pilanesberg did the obvious thing and brought in a bunch of little elephants. This seemed to be a wonderful solution to a double problem—no elephantss in Pilanesberg and too many in the Kruger National Park, where the bulldozer component was getting out of hand. Kruger management had been forced to cull to prevent the Park from being turned into homogenous grassland, and it's a soul-searing thing to cull elephants. Well, to cull anything, but elephants in particular. But now, the wisdom of the day said, at least the babies could be spared, and shipped to Pilanesberg.

The result was that a group of young elephants were taken from the area they knew and placed in a strange environment without the guidance of a mature animal to show them the ropes. That's already setting the scene for an elephantine version of *Lord of the Flies* before we even mention the fact that these littlies had just witnessed the mass murder of their entire family groups.

Galloping to the rescue came Randall Moore, an American who had bought two adult female African elephants from a circus in the States with the sole intention of releasing them into the wild in Africa. These mature ladies were introduced to the desperate youngsters, and to everyone's relief, they all settled down. A strong matriarchal presence seem to pull the little ones into line and give them the comfort and security they needed.

But it wasn't the entire solution. Ten years later the now pubescent youngsters began displaying aberrant, even delinquent, behaviour. The young bulls, being the only bulls around, came into musth at a remarkably young age, and stayed in musth for extraordinarily long periods. Adolescent males are pushed out of the female groups to go and fend for themselves, and they usually attach themselves to a bachelor group somewhere and hang out with the guys. Only there weren't any big guys to hang out with.

So once again, the youngsters felt abandoned. Being in an abandoned mood when you're stoked to the eyebrows with testosterone is a recipe for disaster. A few tourist cars were pushed around. Finally a tourist was killed by an enraged adolescent, and it was obvious that this was more than just a phase the elephants were going through. And then came the ravages on rhinos. In three years, forty white rhinos lost their lives in uneven sparring matches with adolescent elephants. That was a loss of four million Rand at the day's rhino prices.

Obviously the answer was to bring in some big guys. Have you any idea how big a big elephant is? On the gate-post of the boma at Pilanesberg, where the big males were housed before release, are marked the shoulder height of each of the six big bulls that were brought in. Take two well-built young wildlife rangers, each over six foot tall, get the one to hoist the other in the air by providing a stirrup with his hands, and the

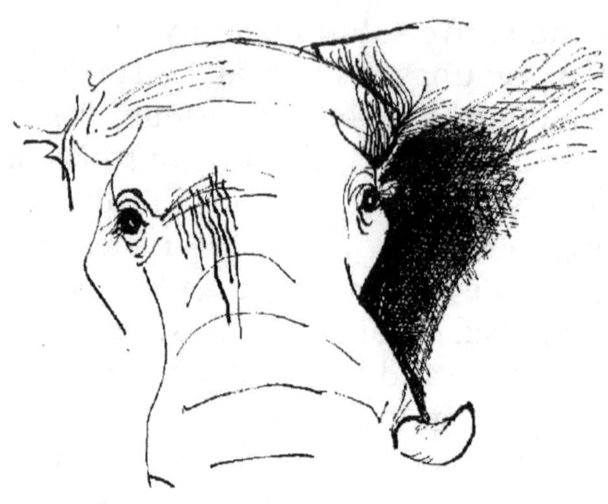

man in the air will have to stretch to his utmost to reach the mark of just the second tallest elephant. I know, because I watched them try. A mature male elephant is absolutely huge.

Which is why no-one had ever tried to translocate an adult bull elephant before. Luckily a cement company with an elephant as their logo found this too good an opportunity to miss, and supplied the wherewithal to build special trucks for the purpose, and just over a year ago [i.e. 1998] the group of bulls were introduced to Pilanesberg National Park.

Since then there have been no untoward happenings, and although the adolescent males are sporting a few obvious bruises and scrapes through correctional action by their elders and betters, the remaining rhinos are—so far—leading an untroubled existence.

For me, having survived the seduction of the feminist movement with my admiration of males most unfashionably intact, this seems to be a vindication.

The big guys will always be essential to a balanced society, whether it seems politically correct or not.

Elephant Lady
10th May

One of the great delights of reporting on wildlife is meeting the scientists who actually know about these things. Inevitably they are fascinating people, and often their personal story is as riveting as the wildlife they study.

Take Dr Marion Garaï[4], for instance, Chair of the Elephant Management and Owners Association since its inception five years ago (i.e. 1994). Swiss born, Marion was schooled both in Zimbabwe and in Switzerland, and the mind-boggling gap between the two styles and levels of education led the bewildered lass into believing that school was a waste of time. So she joined the theatre at the age of sixteen, and launched into a very successful career on the stage. (If

---

[4] 2016: Dr M E Garaï is currently Chair of the Elephant Specialist Advisory Group.

this is sounding singularly unscientific—just be patient, all will be revealed.)

We would probably never have known that Marion existed at all if her dog hadn't died. In an attempt to fill the aching gap that he left in her life, Marion wandered down to the Zürich Zoo and found herself in front of the elephant enclosure.

"They chose me," she says.

Day after day she watched the Asian elephants in their enclosure and more and more she became aware that she was being invited to study them.

So, at the age of 36, she decided to go back to school and complete a university entrance matric. It took her three years, doing two years at a time, and she had to learn Italian as a third language, but she did it, and enrolled at Zürich University to study zoology.

"That was sheer joy after the grind of matric," she muses, and it must have been. She sailed through an honours course, and followed it with a Masters, studying behaviour in captive Asian elephants. Then she came out to South Africa for her PhD in elephant ethology at Pretoria University. Specifically, this lean slightly-pixie-looking female studied the behaviour of translocated wild elephants.

It was tough going, studying nervous elephants out in the bush. Apart from having to get along with the elephants, Marion had to get along with the people involved in similar or allied areas of work—an almost exclusively male world. And if you think a Swiss actress might just perhaps prove to be a little frail and emotional in the savage African bush, think again. She thrived.

And the elephants must be delighted with their choice. Marion has proved to be a clear thinking, logical and acute observer.

"It's not so very different from being an actor, you know," she says. "My business has always been the observation and analysis of behaviour. As an actress I focussed on people. Now it's elephants."

Miraculously she manages to steer clear of the hysteria that usually accompanies elephant-hugging behaviour in females, and she has written guidelines on elephant management which have been adopted by at least one regional wildlife agency in South Africa as part of their management policy.

With the welfare of elephants always uppermost in her mind, one would expect her to live as close as possible to these huge and lovable creatures. When I asked her where the elephants were on her charming little game and guest-farm in the Waterberg, she smiled and said,

"I have enough space here to keep perhaps one third of one elephant. Which third would you suggest?"

Africa Burning
Zambia, 3rd June

In winter, the whole of Africa seems to burn. There are arresting land-sat photographs showing successive lines of fire sweeping inland from the northern Mozambique coast, throwing white smoke streamers before them like oriental ribbon dancers. To windward the view of the land is crystal clear, striped black on the brown August veld; ahead the wind carries the smoke into a milky wash that gradually obscures the ground. This part of Africa has been affected minimally by modern man. Perhaps this is a window on the pattern of fire in Africa's past.

Travelling into Kafue National Park in Zambia's golden mid-winter, just such a wash of pallid fragrant smoke rolled slowly over the road. Far from being the 'pall' so frequently described, with all its suggestions of death and grieving, it was a phenomenon of fullness and opportunity. The fire was moving slowly towards us, encouraged by a gentle breeze, and the sound of crackling was clearly audible. Ahead of us the road had become a veritable buffet for birds. Keeping one hop ahead of the fire were a myriad of insects, and as they landed on the smooth surface of the road, the birds would scoop down and pick them off. Fork tailed drongos and lilac breasted rollers were the most enthusiastic feeders, black kites swooped and swayed in and out of the smoke to catch the larger grasshoppers and locusts, but hornbills and robins and glossy starlings also took advantage of the mobile feast.

As soft flakes of ash spiralled down, we sat spellbound by this reminder that fire is not always an instrument of destruction.

Waves of ten foot high elephant grass (*Pennisetum purpureum*) enclosing the road burst into incandescence as the fire reached it. The thick bases of their cane-like stems popped like firecrackers in the heat, but were still too green to burn completely. Whole patches were left unburned, with trees and shrubs untouched.

We slept out that night on the edge of a grassy dambo, and woke to a mist-shrouded dawn, our canvas bedcovers soaked with dew, to find the fierce flames extinguished by the cold and damp.

Fire, rather like vultures, hyena and wild dog, has had a bad press.

Because it is so obviously an instrument of change, it is seen as A Bad Thing. But besides causing a minor feeding frenzy for the birds, the rolling wave of regeneration consumes the dry, grassy over-burden and discarded autumn leaves and transforms nutrients trapped in them into ash, now accessible to nourish new growth. Grass is designed to be stripped of its leaves, and such a removal stimulates a regeneration from the rootstock. Within a week or so, if there is enough moisture left in the soil from the summer rains, there will be a green flush showing through the blackened stubble. That's a sight to delight the heart of any grazer, especially after a month of rather stale and juiceless fodder.

Driving through a patchy burn a few weeks later, we saw two groups of pointy-faced Lichtenstein's hartebeest gently nosing their way through the sooty veld. It took me a long time to realise that the darker markings on their flanks were not a real coat-colour difference, but a transference of soot from their muzzles to their sides as they stopped nibbling lush green shoots and swiped at irritating flies. They certainly didn't regard the fire as bad news. They were fat, shiny and obviously thriving.

Zambia is an endless sea of tall woodlands, broken dramatically here and there by vast treeless wetlands, glorious grassy dambos spreading into the woodlands like fingers. Fire in Zambia's proclaimed parks is forbidden, but ironically there exists an official national policy of promoting the early burning of its woodlands. Late fires, around October when everything is really dry, are very hot and all-consuming. 'Cool' early burns protect woody plants by reducing the quantity of tinder-dry grass and dead material, and forming patchy natural fire-breaks here and there.

So, although veld fires are illegal in the park, a spread of small early burns reduces the occurrence of large hot later burns which can be so destructive. But the question of whether to allow it to happen or not is mostly academic, since National Parks staff simply lack the means to prevent or extinguish fires anyway.

Playing with fire
7th June

One of the interesting anomalies about conservation is the typically human desire to have things stay the same. A stretch of bushveld that looks like it did a century ago is seen as 'well conserved'. It's a trap we all fall into, this thought that if something looks the same year after year, that is how it should be. Not so. In nature, if something doesn't change, it's dead.

Life is dynamic, change is inevitable and necessary. Lack of change may be comforting for us conservative humans, but it is just one step ahead of decay. Which itself is simply change.

An area set aside to be used by man for recreational purposes, like a game reserve, has to be managed, whether fenced or not. It cannot be regarded as 'natural' since it no longer functions as it did before man isolated it, or surrounded it with cities, villages or farms. Keeping things as untrammelled and wild as possible, or 'as they were' takes careful management and manipulation. And if the management is too rigid, it might result in damage of a different sort.

Take fire, for instance. I'm all in favour of a good veld burn—now and then. It's a natural phenomenon, caused back in the mists of time by lightning or volcanoes. More recently early man used it to improve his hunting chances; fire would clear the vegetation so he could see further, and it could also be used to drive game in a desired direction. And after the burn, new shoots would attract game allowing good hunting opportunities. Great tool, fire.

When it came to cultivation, well, fire was good for getting rid of all the stuff you didn't want so you could plant the stuff you did. Unfortunately, this is where the problems start. Once you start planting things, you've got to hang around, chase the birds and the game off the incipient harvest, and put down roots yourself to gather the rewards. So man became more settled and more numerous, with more and more livestock.

Staying in one place meant having to stimulate more green grazing for domestic stock too. Burning the dry grass will do that. That is, as long as there is enough moisture in the ground to stimulate a flush of new shoots, and as long as there are not so many grazers that the grass has to regenerate from root reserves again and again before the rains come. If that happens, you exhaust the plant and you kill the grass. That's what over-grazing is all about. Africa is mostly over-grazed. And over-burned. Repeated burning will eliminate many of the plant species, which leads to loss of food resources, loss of habitat, and loss of biodiversity.

Yet there are plants that will only regenerate through fire. Protea seed for example will only germinate after a fire. Horticulturists have found they can stimulate germination by blowing quantities of smoke through the seed heads. Many plants have evolved mechanisms like multi layered outer-coatings to stems, which can flame off and leave the working bark untouched. Creatures too have adapted to fire, like the *Lycaenid* butterflies, who form an association with ants. In exchange for a sugary substance, the butterfly larvae are taken into the anthills and out of the reach of fire, emerging in time to eat the new green flush after the winter scorching. Fire is a natural phenomenon.

It's all a matter of balance, which is what poor old mankind is not so good at. But we are learning. In Pilanesberg National Park, for instance, there is a very carefully controlled veld burning programme. What makes it so extraordinary is that the pattern of burning is deliberately random. No area has the same burn twice.

It gets to sound rather Zen-like; the best control appears to be maximum control aping no control at all. The mind boggles! Sooner or later biologists are going to become leaders in philosophy.

Lake Kashiba
Zambia, 14th June

We drove out on a damply overcast Saturday in January—the height of the rainy season—past the little towns of Kapiri Mposhi and Kabwe, the edge of the old Copper-belt, into Mpongwe, best farming district in

Zambia because of the abundance of lime in the region—a natural fertiliser.

The limestone sinkhole or doline that forms Lake Kashiba is beside St Anthony's Mission, and the prettiest (and easiest) part of the trip was the road to the Mission itself. The main road had been graded just before the rains, and the loosened surface dissolved into a glutinous orange mud almost axle deep in places. Much of the journey was spent slithering sideways, peering through a thick mist of mud spots that plated the windows. But the road to St Anthony's Mission had been miraculously ignored and was in good firm condition.

Rinsing the mud off our windscreen revealed rich park-like forests and a wealth of wild flowers:—salmon pink and butter yellow drifts of parrot-beak gladioli, each coyly down-curved petal marked, like a scientific drawing, with a delicate tracery of maroon spots, banks of indigenous begonias, icing sugar pink among lush moss and flourishing ferns—fragile white spider lilies with leaves folded and creased like paper fans.

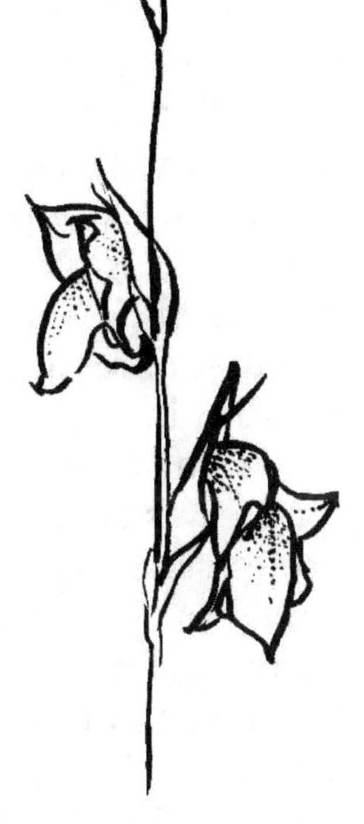

The Lake itself is a proclaimed Natural Monument, and is locally well known. Deservedly so. About 80 metres in diameter, the Lake lies just below ground level, neither drawing from nor feeding a little marshy stream that wanders past. Water the colour of antique glass goes down forever into a well of elephant-grey rock, overhung with graceful swampy bush and huge trees festooned with lianas. A well-mannered official took a modest camping fee and sent off our rather unwelcome, exuberantly noisy, self-appointed guides from the Mission.

There are no facilities. We slept on the roof of the Landy, and were woken at four in the morning, just as the rain stopped threatening and got on with it in earnest. It wasn't the rain which woke us, but a weird and startling cry that sounded like a cross between a manic-depressive night-bird and a sexually active windmill.

This wheezing, whistling, thumping, climactic gurgle was taken up and repeated five or six times from around the Lake, each call dying away before a reply would build out of the cloud-blacked deadness of the damp night. A wonderful sound. The sort of sound that Spielberg would give his right arm to have invented— or maybe George Lucas for the Star Wars soundtrack— only neither of them could possibly use it, since it sounds far too lunatic to be believable.

We puzzled about it right through our rain-soaked breakfast and soggy departure for Lusaka. It must have been a mammal, since no bird has a larynx complex enough to cope with that, though the vocal sounds could be augmented by air-pouches and foot-thumping. We asked around on our return and finally found a biologist who was prepared to venture an opinion.

"Tree dassie," he said complacently, "That's what you heard. Sounds like something disgusting having its throat slit."

He described how they call singly, in the small hours of the morning, in roll-call fashion, so I'm sure he's right. None of the books that I've looked at since have quite managed to describe that weird call, but I suppose if one spends one's life looking like a featureless, rather blandly round-edged dassie, almost as forgettable as one's boulder-based cousins and

nocturnal to boot, it might be nice to have a really electrifying call.

One other remarkable memory lingers from that soggy weekend. On the way to Kabwe we saw the ubiquitous roadside vendors with spread mats displaying voluptuous heaps of rich orange-red; piles of crimson and saffron like the gathered flakes of an African sunset. Trusting that whatever is for sale to the locals by the locals must be safely edible, we stopped and bought ourselves four generous handfuls of this unknown but irresistibly glowing gourmet's delight.

The fact that the food is a fungus gave me a few insecure moments, but we bravely cooked and ate them with a great deal of relish and a fair quantity of grit, these scarlet little funnel-shaped fungi called locally "citondo". They were very good, like highly flavoured if rather sand-textured mushrooms. Botanist Mike Bingham tells me the Latin name is *Cantharellus cibarius*, "And it's just a chantarelle," he says nonchalantly, as if eating bright red fungi is the most natural thing in the world. But these are the sort of surprises that make Zambia such a joy.

Footnote relating to plants
Zambia, 21st June

It's my firm belief that a handicap is a huge advantage in life. Certainly it has been so in mine. Somehow I never learned to stand on my own feet until circumstances deprived me of half of one of them. Suddenly I found my feet. Maybe, like cartoon cat Garfield, I didn't know I had them.

Not being able to take simple things, like feet, for granted opened up vast new areas of awareness I'm sure I would have been blind to otherwise. Since I have to watch where I put them, I see far more of the minutia of nature than the grand sweeping views. That's a great benefit. The panoramas will still be there when I come to a halt, but the tiny things once missed seem gone forever. I have met a glorious array of divine insects, minor mammals, little reptiles, decorative spiders and fascinating caterpillars in this way. Not to mention intriguing rocks, stone age implements and wonderful plants.

On this last score, Zambia contains a plethora of glorious plants that are entirely new to me. Naturally a lot of them are shared by Zimbabwe and Malawi, but many of them are not seen as far down the continent as the South African highveld ridge that has mostly been my home. And being generally a wetter country than either Zimbabwe or South Africa, Zambian plant growth is often much lusher and more impressive. Elephant grass, for instance. You vanish without trace in that stuff, ten foot tall is not an exception. It's one of the *Pennisetums*—those found in South Africa are of a much more humble stature. But the most startling plant I've seen hardly looked like a plant at all.

We were trundling in a sedate manner through hilly country, wending our four-wheeled way down to the Luangwa River, where I hoped to see the largest carpentry tool in Africa. A giant sander, carved out of the hillside itself. This is the final step in producing a really neat (in the original sense of the word) looking makorro, or dug-out canoe. Once all the actual boat-shaping has been done, by hand with an adze, the exterior needs to be smoothed down. And if you don't have sand paper, you just use sand. Better still, sand and rock. And gravity, the ultimate labour saving device. Generations of makorro builders have used this natural slip-way down an incline into the water. A few trips down there in the makorro, and all the rough bits are smoothed away. Must be a tooth-jarring ride, but exhilarating. As we puttered along, looking for a way down to the water that my half-foot could handle, so to speak, I suddenly spotted something that looked for all the world like a broken wine-bottle, with its neck thrust into the sand. It was in an old disused field and bereft of any vegetation, so it was clearly visible. When I saw a second one we decided to stop and investigate.

The thing was a flower. The stem burst leafless from dry ground, and unfurled into a spathe of velvet black, so deep it seemed almost purple. Like a satanic candle, a black spadix rose from the centre, part of it chewed away by some unseen predator. The whole bloom stood about a foot high. I leaned my face over the fluted and ragged edge to see if there was a distinctive scent, and discovered the base of the dark cup to be full to the brim with tiny brown beetles. These could be what had munched the flower, but it looked more like the tables had turned and the flower was munching back. Perhaps it was a carnivorous plant?

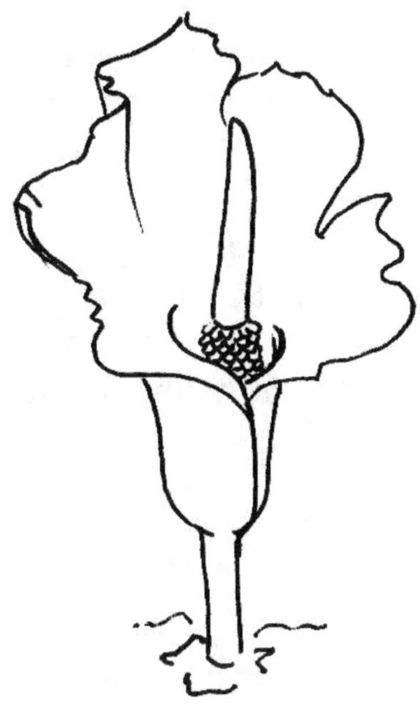

Lusaka's plant boffin, Mike Bingham, knew immediately what it was we had seen.

"It's the black arum, *Amorphophallus abyssinicus*," we were told. And no, it's not a sort of a Venus fly-trap (despite the allure of a morphing phallus allied to Venus). The presence of the myriad beetles remains a bit of a mystery. Presumably they are the pollination agents. What attracts them I can't guess, since there seemed no scent at all. Maybe the flower tastes delicious to beetles, despite its poisonous levels of oxalic acid. The absence of a leaf was diagnostic too, since the black arum only sends up a single, much divided leaf after the flower has died back. The plants are said to be found in woodland and in rocky areas, on or near the base of termite mounds, and flower early in the rainy season. It was late November when we saw them.

I was so delighted with this extraordinary plant that it was more than compensation for our failure to find a way for me to view the giant sanding-machine. Another triumph for the footlet.

Mike Bingham
28th June

It is quietly thrilling to know personally someone who has had a creature or a plant named for them. So it gives me great pleasure to introduce you to an extraordinary person who has achieved this honour no less than five times, with Bingham's termite, *Mimeutermes binghami*; Bingham's butterfly *Charaxes ethalion* subsp. *Binghami*; two species of fig tree pollinating wasps, *Alfonsiella binghami* and *Platyscapa binghami*; and Bingham's amaryllis *Crinum binghamii*.

Michael Graham Bingham is what used to be called a naturalist. More than being an adequate all-rounder, he is an all-round Specialist. But plants are his big thing right now, and if one were to describe him as a botanical specimen, it would sound something like this:

"*Bingham michaelis grahamii.* The genus Bingham is South African in origin, but this particular species has taken to Zambian soil with such enthusiasm that one might be forgiven for thinking it endemic to the area. Of a neat, compact but vigorous growth, this hardy evergreen is characterised by silvery foliage, somewhat fine and feathery, and rather reminiscent of *Einstein albertii*. Found mainly in the woodland understory in remote rural areas where it appears happiest, it can nevertheless be found even in urban gardens, and is frequently associated with agriculture."

Most unplantlike, Mike gets around a great deal. He is probably one of the most energetic people I've met. He thinks nothing of diving off on a three mile hike through his divinely jungley garden to share some obscure botanical treasure. Admittedly, it may not have been all of three miles, but the denseness of the growth and the dimness of the filtering green-and-dappled light sifting through tall trees made it feel like a veritable bit of bush-whacking though romantic Darkest Africa. As a result my admiration of the single intricate leaf of the *Amorphophallus* was rather

breathless, but within seconds Mike had whirled off on another topic and was plunging off again through the thicket to find something else he wanted to share.

Random and rapid movement is as much mental as physical in Mike. His brain is twice as agile as his frame, grasshoppering from one topic to another, highlighting sudden gleaming facets of riveting detail before leaping on to another subject. The magical garden he and his wife Trish developed is as surprising and as exciting. Seemingly random, there is a pattern or logic that I couldn't grasp and Mike knows exactly where everything is. He has employed great skill and understanding in coaxing reluctant wild vegetation into fecund garden abundance.

Another plunge through the almost under-sea green and we emerged on the brink of a picture perfect little farm, neat rows of rhubarb and Swedish kale, aubergines glowing richly in the morning sunshine, and an orchard of litchis with ripe fruit russet-red against glossy dark leaves. Beautiful. Such a contrast. This is Trish's domain, and shows her clarity and order. Vibrant life and growing things seem to be the abiding passion of their lives, and even their home is centred on growing things. The Japanese-simple glass-fronted lounge is edged by a veranda joyous with clay pots. Wooden sculptures peep shyly through cascading curtains of leaves, and even the veranda furniture breathes rich Africa, with an entanglement of cast-iron wildlife and gloriosa lilies.

The garden somehow is encouraged in through this fringing of pots, and permeates the room like the presence of a loved one. Packets of seeds lie on the desk, pots and jars of agri/horti-cultural matter are dotted about among a blizzard of books which lie like leaf-litter on every surface. Fat and beautiful baskets remind one of seed-pods, bursting with unknown contents. The books seem almost organic, reaching up to the ceiling like a forest, towers of books, serried ranks, vast soaring boles of book-trees sweep upward, and among them are brilliant glowing patches of colour like snatches of sunlight. These are Trish's watercolour paintings—also vibrant with the greenly growing glory of nature.

Hidden talents seem to be characteristic of both Binghams. A little gentle delving unearths the fact that Mike played the clarinet before that talent got buried in a welter of matters animal, vegetable and mineral. He shares his wife's artistic eye, and specialised in the difficult art of macro-photography. His superb photographic histories of butterfly and moth life-cycles grace publications of international repute. One detects a slight residual hint of regret in the forthright relief he proclaims at having left that particular enthusiasm behind.

These more introspective thoughts were shared over a succulent lunch prepared by Mike's own hands—oyster mushrooms sautéed in butter, crisp ears of sweet-corn (nuked, to my horror, in the microwave) and glowing sun-warmed tomatoes served as nature intended. A few litchis rounded off a very satisfying meal, washed down with a cup of honey-sweetened tea large enough to be termed a dish. Somehow these gentle domestic skills are a little surprising in a man who is scientist clean through to the bone. He gained his degree in Chemistry and Zoology at the University of Natal, and went on to do his Honours Degree in Zoology there. His first job however employed him as an entomologist, and by 1995 his botanical expertise saw him a Research Associate of the Missouri Botanical Garden in the United States of America. He was pivotal in setting up a Botanical Trust aimed at establishing a national herbarium and botanic garden for Zambia, and his intense interest in the country's natural wealth is boundless.

July, 1999

The behaviour of the black collared barbets in my garden once again proves that they don't read the books. The Big Book of Birds (*The Complete book of Southern African Birds*, Struik-Winchester 1989) says these "enter gardens and breed there, but they are wary and uncommon visitors to bird tables". My barbets think they own the food table. And since it's a small hop from there to the carefully strung up nesting log, maybe they have a right to feel a little proprietorial about it.

There used to be three in my garden group, the original pair and the offspring from the first year in the nesting log. All three of them hung about and shared the nest for the second season, and since this is just outside my office window, I could hear a second brood of little ones learning that the squeaky wheel gets the grease.

And suddenly it stopped. One day there was utter silence. The three adults hung around for a while, behaving in a  rather erratic fashion, and then they left.
Soon after that I became aware of a rat in my roof, and I suspect that the scuffling feet were powered by barbet-chicks. The rat—and the fellow who moved in to take his place—were both dispatched (with Racumin, an owl-friendly poison) and slowly the barbets came back. I only see two at a time now, but they're showing interest in the nesting log again so maybe there'll be a few more rustling little squeaks soon.

When I was up in Zambia's Kafue National Park in June I saw a black collared barbet that blew my mind. Its belly was bright, clear yellow. The Big Book says the belly is whitish; Roberts' (*Roberts' Birds of Southern Africa*) sixth edition, published by the John Voelcker Bird Book Fund) says "dull pale yellowish-grey". I've seen a photograph of a black collared barbet with a yellow spot on its tummy, but the Kafue bird was road-marking yellow. The knowledgeable wildlife boffin with me said, "Don't be silly, they ALL look like that," but went on to talk about the total irrelevance of colour variations anyway.

On getting back to Pretoria I spoke to Anthony van Zyl at the Transvaal Museum, who is their barbet man (and an expert on kestrels). Anthony is reputed to look like Jaluka singer, Johnny Clegg. I couldn't say, since I've not seen Johnny Clegg in the flesh. But there is no doubt that Anthony has more than a hint of the raffishly romantic in his features—blue eyes and wild dark hair. Apparently he also has an interesting tattoo about his person, and idly speculating exactly where that might be tends to distract me from our conversation, so I prefer to talk to him over the phone.

Anthony tells me that there is a subspecies of black collared barbets in the Kafue area called *pumilio* which have clear yellow bellies, but that these are paler than the more western subspecies *bocagei*, which have really bright yellow bellies. I asked if the colour was influenced by diet, and Anthony seems to think it might, but it's also a matter of breeding groups bringing out a dominant gene. Apparently there is considerable variation both in colour and in size, resulting in a classification of seven subspecies altogether.

Remarkable when one thinks that the distribution of the black collared barbet is only from the Eastern Cape to northern Tanzania, and excluding a bit of Namibia. Anthony tells me there is a rare yellow-headed variety found "northwards", which is about as vague as possible. I'll let you know if I ever see one.

Or his tattoo.

Hamerkop
12th July

Sitting quietly one afternoon in Kafue National Park in Zambia, watching nothing in particular along the forested fringe of the Lufupa River, we witnessed an extraordinary thing. Suddenly rising from the leaf canopy was a group of about a dozen birds—I thought there were nine, my scientific advisor thought it was closer to thirteen. And they played in the wind off the water. Flying in single-file, the first bird would drive into the updraft and then glide, letting the wind sweep it up and backwards in a graceful arc over the heads of the others, till it had slowly dropped into the tail of the queue, neatly taking up position behind the rest.

This amazing game was like a giant avian Ferris wheel, each bird coasting up on the breeze and gliding backwards in slow motion to join the back of the line again. The spectacle lasted less than a few minutes, and the birds vanished back into the canopy of the forest strip just as suddenly as they had appeared. It had all been done in silence, in a wind that didn't reach us, and to add to our sense of general disbelief, the birds were hamerkops.

I have never seen more than two hamerkops together, and I've always thought of them as essentially solitary birds. It seems that they are, and they are not. Turns out that no-one is entirely sure about hamerkops, not even the ornithologists. For a start the birds are so peculiar that they have only one species in their entire genus and are something of an embarrassment to science, generally being slotted into the bird books somewhere between the storks and herons, though they are not much like either. When I phoned my favourite bird authority, Dr Alan Kemp at the Transvaal Museum, he pointed out that apart from work done in West Africa concerning hamerkops in

conjunction with rice farming, nobody has studied them.

"There are a lot of birds we don't know much about," Alan confided, "mouse-birds are another, and grey louries. Spend a week studying one of them and you will be the world expert on the subject."

So if you've always wanted to be an expert on something, take a week off and study the hamerkop. It's a tempting idea, really, since hamerkops are so very oddly behaved. Take their nests for instance. These are massive constructions of mud and sticks and a variety of debris piled into a great heap. It resembles nothing so much as the aftermath of a flood trapped in the fork of a tree. Actually, it's not always in a tree, sometimes it's on a ledge of rock, but it's almost always above a stream or a river. This huge mud mansion is scruffy on the outside, and carefully wood-panelled with sticks on the inside. It takes about six weeks to complete, which is a huge investment in bird terms, and appears to be regarded as one of the most desirable residences in the bush. There have been occasions when poor old hamerkop doesn't even get the chance to finish the thing before squatters move in.

The giant eagle owl for instance likes to take over the establishment before the roof goes on, since he (or she) is too big to squeeze in once that happens, but they are also happy to live on top. Barn owls on the other hand will take it over at any stage, regardless of whether there are eggs or even chicks in the nest. To the barn owl, it just means taking over a house with a well-stocked larder. Monitor lizards, pythons, kestrels, Egyptian and knob billed geese, even bees find it an almost irresistible home. And it lasts for years and years. Which is another puzzle. Because the hamerkop builds a new one every year. Sometimes.

I'm told that the hamerkop also has the occasional curious habit of dancing. A small group of birds will get together with "excited calling and tremulous squawking" says the Big Bird Book. The dance consists of what sounds like a variant of Dr Seuss' Hop on Pop, with one bird standing on another's back.

"They're not copulating," says Allan, "they are just standing there. After a while the top bird hops down and they stand side by side, and another bird hops up. It's very odd."

That's a comment you'll hear again and again when you're talking about hamerkops. It is very odd. Which is why it features so strongly in local folklore. Yet, apart from its distinctive hammer-head, it's an undistinguished looking bird. Perhaps it's making up for a fairly drab exterior with psychedelic behaviour? Whatever it's motivation, it's a plum project just begging for a student with a bit of time.

The Nightjar's Comb
19th July

Some people say nature leaves them cold. They look at a vista of breeze-combed grass and a scattering of thorn trees, and they say, "But it's empty! There is nothing to look at!" Excitement is lots of people, shopping malls and entertainment. Movies, displays and stage shows are essential parts of life to some, yet they mostly rely on fooling the viewer, making things look more desirable, more intriguing, more attractive, more "real" than they are. If you look closely, you see the window-dresser's pins, the cleverly positioned light source, the cardboard made to look like granite or gold, the scarcely believable flight of fancy.

The fascination of nature is that the closer you look the more intricate the details are, and the more astounding. Take for example the case of the nightjar's comb.

I had heard of this phenomenon but had never seen it, and when I asked a student ornithologist about it some years ago, got a blank stare and a shrug of the shoulders. I had written it off as something I had misunderstood. Even without a comb, nightjars are interesting. The scientific name alone is fascinating.

Caprimulgus comes from the Latin for goat—'capri' (as in Capricorn) and mulgus meaning 'to milk'. The old English name for them is Goat-suckers. Like tick-birds the name was given by semi-observant farming people jumping to conclusions. Nightjars were known to hang around goat pens in the twilight so they must be stealing milk, just as egrets were seen to be hanging around cattle so they must be eating ticks.

The birds are not guilty on both counts. What they are doing is watching for insects disturbed by the animals. Egrets do this by day, but nightjars feed in the twilight squatting on the ground, staring up into the sea-green light to see the insects. Then they fly up with mouths agape—and this is the other reason for their strange English name—they have huge mouths. Big enough to suck milk out of a goat. This avian scoop-net is surrounded by a fringe of stiff bristles, which I suppose work rather like a cat's whiskers—the bird can feel an insect even when just out of eyeshot, and move the beak to intercept it.

The shape of the bird's head is constructed to cope with this method of feeding. The rather big eyes

are set a little higher on the head than most birds, making gazing upward easier, and the wide mouth almost splits the head in two. Our glimpses of nightjars are usually only as a pathetic little bundle of cryptic feathers left in the road. The bird's habit of lying in a conveniently open patch of ground, like a road, to have an unobstructed view of the dawn or dusk sky, results in a lot of road kills. The skull is very thin and fragile, and even if neither the car nor the bird are moving very fast, the bird is inevitably killed.

And so it was at twilight, as we motored down to the Luangwa, that we had a head-on collision with a nightjar. We stopped and picked up the little corpse, a bundle of soft speckled feathers. As I turned the sad warm remains over in my hand, I suddenly saw it. The comb!

On the centre toe of each foot, the claw is modified into a delicate comb. It really does exist. No-one knows exactly what it is for, but it's thought that the birds use it to groom those sensitive whiskers on either side of the beak. I'm told that Des Jackson is the world expert on nightjars, and when I track him down I'll tell you more.

That's what I mean about intricate details, and the wonder of nature; there is always more to explore, more to discover.

Leaving Pretoria
25th July

Things have been a little frantic in what passes for the Dacombe home. Pretoria has been my base for over a decade, and I've developed a very deep, if unfashionable, affection for the city. Now we're off to Malawi for a few years, and I decided it was time for a complete change. So I'm selling up the base in the interests of greater mobility.

Certainly there are aspects of Pretoria I won't miss. Theft, for example. This seems to be almost a national sport throughout South Africa—in fact much of Africa in general. I was amused to find that the one place that can boast a zero crime rate is Robben Island! Last week my rather nice mountain bike grew legs, and a few days later the chaps came back and relieved me of my computer. No point in making a song and a dance about it, both occasions were the result of personal carelessness. But the loss of my old Cyclops hits very hard. Apart for costing me time, in pretty short supply right now with the road to Malawi beckoning, it has cost me a treasure hoard of accumulated data. Serve me right for not keeping back-ups.

One of the most painful losses is a checklist of the birds of Pretoria that my son John was working on. It was still in the process of being rechecked and verified, but John and his associate at the Pretoria Zoological Gardens, Brendan Boyes, had identified about 380 species of birds in the city limits. That's pretty impressive by any standard, and is one of the reasons I've become so fond of this place.

According to Alan Kemp at the Transvaal Museum, this huge array of avifauna is the result of the city perching between several disparate ecosystems. There are the remnants of highveld grasslands south and east, almost completely replaced by suburban garden-forest; the Magaliesberg mountain system westward, and the bushveld complex to the north. Where these areas overlap, or change from one to another, one finds birds which prefer one or other of the areas all in the same place.

In the garden of my little house which shelters in the sub-suburb of Clydesdale, under the towering walls of the local Mecca—the Loftus rugby stadium— almost in the heart of central Pretoria, I have seen spotted creeper, golden tailed woodpecker, grey headed shrike and a purple heron. Not all on the same day, of course, and not only these few. I've even seen a very shy looking European cuckoo, being reviled by a loud-mouthed boubou. On our cycling tours de Clydesdale we've rubber-necked at a wryneck, and discovered the day nest of the spotted dikkop in the grounds of Girls High. We've even stopped thunderstruck, while hanging washing in the backyard, at the unmistakable call of the fish-eagle.

There are the more conventional citizens of my garden too, the prolific thrush family, who seem to produce fat teddy-bear chicks in twins twice a year, leaving the parents looking unbelievably scruffy and desperate. The prosperous and glossy Cape robin  nesting in the ivy, who cheerfully composes grocery lists morning and evening ('we need cornflakes.... aaaand... a box of tea bags... aaaaand.... two pound of butter.... aaaand...'), the glorious hoopoe, more frequently seen in winter but always with a sharp delight at the thoroughly African drama of its plumage, and of course the dynasty of black collared barbets, whose daily saga I have followed like a soap-opera for years whenever I've been at home. These I will miss.

But there is no escaping the fact that since the arrival of the Indian minahs the neighbourhood has deteriorated. What a noisy and ill-mannered bunch of squatters they are! They tour around the parks and pavements in squadrons of four, terrorising crested barbets and shouting abuse at all and sundry. Listening to them settling down at night in their communal roost gives the clearest idea of their lack of breeding. The jostling and swearing gradually sinks into a low desultory murmur, when inevitably one bird will shout "Fart! Fart!" and the entire extended family bundles out of the tree amid great hilarity and raucous abuse. Gradually the vulgarity dies down, and they all go back to bed.

Definitely lowering the tone of the place. Yes, time for a change—Malawi in just a week! Picture that! There'll be web-fodder for Africa!

Through Mozambique
10th August

My two recent experiences of Mozambique were so insalubrious that I felt both grateful I'd not known the country prior to the civil war, and unwilling to attempt a third visit. So the suggestion that our route to Malawi should take a slow wander through Mozambique did not exactly kindle enthusiasm in my heart.

However, I'm always willing to be proved wrong, so we set off on a five-day meander up the length of the country from Maputo in the south to Tete in the north. My expectations were justified as far as Maxixe, situated on the coast about half-way between Maputo and Beira—the most memorable moments being provided by a stop to change drivers and have a quiet piddle in the grass.

We drew up just short of a bridge that had taken a beating in the last floods. A sturdy metal ramp had been erected over the breech and looked perfectly sound. Obviously the red warning signs on the bank were just an added precaution. We pulled off the road and hopped nimbly into the bushes for a discreet leak, studiously ignoring the rather vocal disapproval from passengers of a passing bus. It's one of the problems of densely populated countries—one needs to delve deeper into the bush for a bit of privacy.

A few minutes later, feeling less pressured and with clothing neatly adjusted, we emerged from our separate bushes to find a smart imported sedan pulling up. The driver leaned out to us and said in perfect Portuguese-flavoured English,

"You must please be very careful here, there are many mines still from the war," and he waved a languid hand at the red skull-and-cross-bones sign, which now very clearly read *PERIGO MINAS*.

No wonder the entire bus had been horrified. The war in Mozambique ended in 1992, but it wasn't until the Ottawa Ban was signed two years ago, that thought was given to the problem of clearing what was estimated to be tens of thousands of mines.

Making the matter more interesting for us were the very floods that modified the bridge, for they also modified the areas marked as either cleared of mines, or verified as mine fields. The weight of water would have scoured the land, sweeping mines downstream and depositing them who knew where. I felt physically ill.

From Maxixe the landscape steadily regained a little of its original lush forested robustness, but the horror of the mines stayed in my head. The little town of Morrumbene, though, is a picturesque delight. I would have loved to have spent some time exploring—the first time I've felt that anywhere in Mozambique. The charm of the neat organic houses beneath coconut palms did much to obliterate the odour of fear in me. Our third night out we shunned formal camping grounds and camped off the road from Vilanculos towards the Save River. My scientific advisor—an essential piece of equipment for any serious camper—unerringly nosed out a perfect camp site, serene and secluded, where the gentle noises of night held only the infrequent sounds of a distant dog or insomniac rooster. A full moon through a tangle of branches and four species of owl calling (Scops, Barred, Grass, and Spotted eagle owls) gave texture to the velvet of a warm African winter evening.

In this Eden I still went through occasional moments of sheer panic about mines. But in Mozambique that's the gamble you take—you can either stay cheek-by-jowl and nose-to-armpit with everyone else, or you can escape into the rapidly dwindling uninhabited bits of country, and trust that it's not your day to croak. For me as a mature person with nothing left to prove and no dependants any more, the risk was amply balanced by the sense of freedom and unity with the bush.

Post Script 2016—Rats to the Rescue

In 1995 a number of serendipitous threads came together—a young Belgian product designer, who had pet rats as a boy, visited Africa as a student; like many, he was bewitched by the land and the people, and shocked by the ravages of war, particularly the horror of landmines.

Enter the Giant African Pouched Rat, Cricetomys gambianus, *a noble species of vermin, weighting just under a kilogram with a total body length of about 76 cm, more than half of which is tail, and indigenous to the wetter northern parts of Mozambique. Being nocturnal, like any self-respecting rat, its sense of smell is vital to survival. As easy to train as a dog, easier to transport, and cheaper to feed— happy to work for a cheek-full of banana for every mine located—they also have the advantage of being too light to trigger the explosive devices.*

Despite the September 2015 declaration of Mozambique as mine free, there are currently [2016] sixteen of these HeroRATs working in Mozambique. This is a special detail, consigned to clear the land that was once occupied by the Malhazine ammunitions store, spectacularly destroyed in an uncontrolled explosion in 2007, scattering incendiary and explosive devices far and wide. Once the rats have done their job, the land will be transformed into the Malhazine Ecological Park.

My sketch is from a photograph of Bart Weetjens by Xavier Rossi which shows the rat truthfully as a Giant rat, not as a cross between a dwarf fox and a deformed fruit bat as I have.

Aiming for Gorongoza
16th August

Our predilection for the road less travelled cost us an extra two nights in the bush, but since this was accompanied by the kind of jubilant self-satisfaction that comes from meeting a Camel-man-type challenge, it was worth it.

Our fuel was running a little low as we reached Inchope, so we turned right to Nhamatanda to change more dollars into Mozambican Meticais. (We got about 12000 to one US dollar—credit cards and travellers cheques are not readily accepted except in really fancy hotels and at the banks, which are only open between 7:30 and 11:15 during week days.) We needed fuel and bread—good Portuguese bread rolls, fresh fruit and vegetables are readily available for cash in the local markets of any village, and we found the Mozambican people polite, good humoured, helpful and wonderfully un-pushy. Also good is the beer. One local brew is labelled Mac Mahon but is called Dois M (twice M) in Portuguese, and is much to our taste.

With supplies replenished, we studied the maps. Both the AA map and our Shell Touring Atlas show a secondary road from Nhamatanda to the Gorongoza

Park entrance, so that was our obvious choice of less frequented route.

The natural optimism of enthusiastic travellers is, in retrospect, a little startling. Having refuelled ourselves and the vehicle, we set off on the road to Gorongoza's main camp, Chitengo. Or was it? We discussed the matter with several of the locals, and chose to be convinced by those that spoke the most emphatically and pointed the most commandingly. The fact that we have no Portuguese, none of them spoke English, and the strong likelihood that they have never personally been to Chitengo, made absolutely no difference. Off we sailed, our canopied two-wheel-drive-with-diff-lock pick-up thumbing her nose at the appalling condition of the track.

But the road seemed to be improving as it looped through brachystegia woodland. In places the trees had been hacked back for cotton fields or fallow lands. Once or twice we saw an old memorial to the colonial days, concrete signboards proclaiming the area to be the property of a Portuguese cotton company, now long since defunct.

In these woodlands I had my first sight of a bark beehive, looking like an improbable log balanced in the topmost branches of a tree. My scientific advisor (who of course was indispensable to this trip, being mechanic, driver, camp locator & attendant, food sampler and ready reference, not to mention being conveniently self-toting. The fact that the sole reason for this move to Malawi is because he is taking up a contract there as advisor to National Parks is beside the point), my scientific advisor, as I was saying, tells me this method of bee-keeping is used in Zambia and Zimbabwe too. Bark is peeled from the trunks of msasa (*Brachystegia spiciformis*) or munondo trees (*Julbernardia globiflora*) and rolled into a cylinder, the split fastened together with a couple of wooden stakes. The open ends are filled either with a disc of wood like a slice of tree-trunk, or packed with grass and held in place with strips of bark fibre. Roughly patched together, a few enticing holes are left into the dark and hollow interior, and with luck a swarm of bees will discover it and move in.

We saw many over the next few kilometres, but none that looked obviously successful. I would have thought that once the bees have had first refusal of the residence, it would be snapped up by house-hunting birds, but apparently not. Closer investigation of one provided several shongololo shells and nothing else.

Needless to say, the road steadily deteriorated, and after exploring other hopeful tracks twice, several times sensing the presence of the Pungwe River if not actually getting a glimpse of it, we fell victim to the inevitable. The light was fading, and we were sure the river crossing was just ahead—but the black cotton soil, certainly impassable in the wet, had turned the tyre-tracks to dongas leaving just the middlemannetjie, so we drove with two wheels on that and the outside two in the bush, rather like rollerblading along the parallel-bars of a gymnasium. This balancing act was bound to end sooner or later, and had we not been racing the light it might have been later. I set up camp while my advisor applied science to the problem. By the time the tent was up and supper was ready the truck was back four-square on firm ground, and we both were feeling worn-out, but pretty smug at our achievements. And there was a moment of high farce the following morning which made it all worthwhile.

My esteemed adviser, having dug the truck out the night before, saw no point in more digging and chose to squat in a road-rut for his morning ablutions. Serenely watching dawn rise with just his head above road level, he was startled to hear a polite "Good morning, sir," from behind him, followed by the enquiry, "Would you perhaps have any salt for me?"

I managed to find the camera in time to record this interaction between the pot-holed scientist and the only pedestrian seen in 24 hours, but I was laughing so much the photograph is a demurely cryptic blur.

With the light, we found we were only about a kilometre from the Inchope/Gorongosa road, and that there was neither bridge nor pontoon across the Pungwe on the secondary route, so even if we had been on the right track, we would not have reached Gorongoza by nightfall.

Curious travellers are slow to learn. We made the same mistake when we left Gorongoza, taking the secondary route between Guro and Tete, through the one-horse ghost-town of Mandie on the Luenna River. We didn't get to Tete, because Mandie is where the road ends. The rusted hulk of the river pontoon lies high and dry across the road from the tiny town hall.

The moral of the tale is don't always trust maps and atlases to tell you about secondary routes, especially in a country still recovering from sixteen years of devastating war.

And don't go anywhere without a scientific adviser.

Sandy Dacombe Ferrar

Gorongoza National Park I
20th August

I'd been wanting to see Gorongoza for an awfully long time. My sister's husband was chief ecologist there for a number of years before the war, and the letters I received were full of the poetry of the place, an evocative blend of sensual Africa and pioneering adventure.

Like the rest of Mozambique, the park is suffering from a dearth of wildlife. In the dreadful years of prolonged war civilians came close to starvation, and everything was, quite naturally, eaten. Even on this trip, sixteen years later, I saw children at the side of the road selling turtle-doves for the pot. Beside the hunger of the people, there has been devastation from those mines I so loathe—records of maimed elephant are abundant, and I presume anything smaller would probably not survive the blast.

The absence of the larger animals like elephant and buffalo has a particular impact, in that the grass gets unbelievably lush. The impression on nearing the rest camp at Chitengo was of a jungle of tall grass and mlala palms. It gave considerable insight into the everyday life of an ant. My advisor's scientific opinion is that it was very like being a sight-seeing flea on the back of a Husky. Lush and jungly does have a certain charm, but it's like driving through a tunnel of vegetation—you can't see a thing unless it's on the road. And of course, there is almost no game to be seen anyway; the proprietor of the tourism information service at Vilancoulos told us with some asperity.

"They'll take your money and you won't see a thing," she said when we asked if Gorongoza was open to the public. That failed to put us off, since we feel that we can see big game anywhere, but there is only one Gorongoza.

The rest camp cum administration centre has more obvious scars of war. Headquarters to both Renamo and Frelimo, handed back and forth as the tide of hostilities changed, the buildings are mostly hollow shells pock-marked by bullets, squat shattered remnants of neat, if graceless, concrete offices and cottages. Reed ablution blocks have been attached to the outer walls of one of these empty-eyed relics, and are kept clean, with running water, flushing toilets and even hot water from a donkey-boiler. The entire rest camp is impeccably kept, but I found the constant reminders of violence and destruction unnerving. For instance there is a shot-up old Volkswagen Kombi—sans interior, engine or wheels and riddled with bullet holes—which is being used as a sign-board, directing visitors to Reception, Administration and the Camp Ground. It's probably a great idea for a military museum or a paint-ball play-ground, but here I found it horrific. I had to shut my mind to the skull-like buildings and the corpses of dead vehicles, close out these echoes of old agony in order to see the real and abundant beauty that still is Gorongoza.

We chatted briefly to Park Warden/Ecologist Roberto Zohlo, who told us that miraculously no species have been lost, and the tiny remnants of wildlife are beginning to increase their numbers. In time this incredibly fertile, sultry flood plain will once again feed teeming herds of buffalo, wildebeest, waterbuck and all the marvellous spectrum of grass-eating plains game.

On the first day, we drove through endless Tarzan-corridors of grass and fan palms, sometimes mlala, sometimes borassus. While gazing at a

particularly stately bottle-stemmed borassus, trying to make up my mind if there was much of a difference between them and the hyphaene, I suddenly spotted a flash of white feathers. Automatically my mind said "palm-nut vulture" but of course it's the wrong kind of palm, and the reality surprised me even more. A pelican! Even though the borassus palm is sturdier and more robust than the mlala, those fronds hardly look strong enough to hold such a ponderous bird.

While craning around to get a better view of this extraordinary sight, a chilling sound from the dense thicket behind us froze my blood. An agonised, muffled bleat of despair that had us both instantly concerned.

Science muttered quietly, "Could be a young waterbuck with a leopard attached to its nose."

I was almost in tears at the thought that there is nothing one can do about natural predation in a National Park. Even if rescue was legal, the thought of my scientific adviser vanishing into a world of grass and reeds higher than the roof of our truck in order to talk a hungry predator out of lunch did not fill me with confidence. I imagined having to listen to both the agonised bleating of whatever was lunch and the crunching of bones as my adviser became a pre-prandial snack.

But the roof was a good thought, and we hauled ourselves out the windows and onto the protesting cab roof to perhaps get a clearer view and some idea of direction. The call came again, and this time Science caught sight of a movement with the call. He pointed to the top of a borassus palm—another pelican, in fact a chick. A very vocal chick, with a bored looking adult. The antelope-calf-in-distress-impersonation was the chick's way of attempting to get its obviously deaf parent's attention.

Nature has a way of making us mere humans look incredibly silly quite a lot of the time.

Gorongoza National Park 2
25th August

In counterbalance to the notable absence of game, the staff of Gorongoza do their best to please. We were handed a photostat copy of a rather elderly map on arrival, listing the regulations on the reverse—an intimidating series of thou-shalt-nots in both English and Portuguese. Despite its unprepossessing appearance, the map has the currently passable tracks marked with a highlighter, and we found the distances accurate. The tracks themselves are in good condition, so under used that the entire track has become grassed over.

The gesture that most impressed me was loaded with such ancient hospitality that I found it deeply moving. Like all campers at sunset, we settled down and pulled out the scoff-box to begin preparations for supper. Out of the gathering gloom came one of the camp attendants, carrying in his hand the smouldering end of a substantial branch of fire-wood. He laid it down on a small bricked area, and with three or four economical movements piled on a few dry branches, breathed on the rosy glowing lump, and almost instantaneously it blossomed into a cheerful fire. This gift of a cooking fire was, like all truly wonderful gifts, superbly timed and infinitely simple. It struck a fundamental chord resonating right to the roots of civilisation.

The next morning we set out early for Gorongoza's renowned sweeping plains. The Park was shrouded in mist and silent. Gradually the jungley thicket of tall grasses and even taller palms gave way to swathes of emerald green parkland dotted with majestic trees, each like a grand statement. Looming out of the milky cloud came the relics of the fabled "lion houses", the old rest-camp cottages erected before World War II. Concrete slab-built with private game viewing platforms on each flat roof, which the lions soon adopted for their own use, pussy-footing up to study the pattern of prey on the plains before loping off for an easy meal. Most of the houses are gone now, just two have a few walls still upright to mark their demise.

Now the trees too thinned and stopped, leaving just the endless carpet of grassy lawn, on and on and on. At least that's how it seemed to us, cocooned in the cab of the pick-up, moving in a bubble of vision through a world of mist. Through the thick carpet of dew-spangled grass, Egrets had left darker trails as they high-stepped their way after insects. With our vision so limited, we wound down the windows to listen for the abundant water-birds we knew should be here—or any sound of the wilderness. Not a good idea. We were instantly besieged by a shrill hoard of mosquitoes. We rapidly closed the windows, but it took us several frantic minutes to reduce the onslaught to a little drift of small grey corpses before we could relax again.

Frustrating as the mist was for us, it would have provided a positive festival for a visiting arachnologist. Every bush, every shrub, every tree or blade of grass seemed draped in spider webs of any conceivable shape and size, each illuminated by pearls of dew and the watery dawn light.

The mist lifted in time for breakfast, and we spent an Out-of-Africa hour quietly crunching corn-flakes, watching a flock of energetic Yellow-billed storks compete with a few Spoonbills for fish-fry in the marsh. The plains are sweeping, but not really endless, and Mount Gorongoza rose up as a distant back-drop, lilac-blue through the remnants of mist. The thin triple piping of white-faced duck and the hoarse rattle of crowned crane threaded the soft air, and a platoon of white pelicans glided down, stately and ponderous as a squadron of bombers. A myriad skeins of water-birds rose and fell in snaking loops as distant flocks constantly left and returned. A single lonely hippo grunted contentedly, and the evocative call

of the fish-eagle meant that somewhere there must be a stretch of open water. Later we saw a self-important looking osprey, arrogantly unaware of how the markings on his head look like a cyclist's crash-helmet and the streaks on his chest like gravy stains.

Driving back towards camp a tiny reed frog was knocked off his grass perch and landed just inside the window. The entire creature was about the size of my little finger-nail. It was a delicate translucent jade green, impossibly tiny hip-bones tenting the skin of its back like a minute marquee. We assumed he was a youngster, since he was so small and his head seemed proportionately bigger than it should, but most frogs seem half head anyway. Baby or adult he was utterly enchanting. We stopped the car and let him hop from hand to hand for a while, the three of us subjecting each other to intense scrutiny—ours of him certainly less fearfully focussed than his of us.

At last he gave a final mammoth jump, clearing both window and side mirror, and vanished back into the reeds and grass.

The scientific half of our equation called out, most unscientifically, "Good luck, little fellow!"

Indeed he needs it. Hard to speculate on how long such a delicate collection of co-ordinated parts can last in the bush. Those rose-tinged toes no thicker than threads and the perfect eyes, tiny jewels of silver-foil set in Venetian glass—one snap of a fork-tailed drongo's beak and he'd be gone. Seems such a waste of perfection.

A waste of perfection. I think that about sums up Gorongoza—indeed most of Africa where the human animal has outgrown its point of balance.

Hello Malawi
30th August

The two days we lost in our Triple A routes (aimlessly arsing around) to and from Gorongoza meant less time to nose around Lilongwe, and my adviser plunged straight into the technicalities and processes of the job he'd come to do, while I spent more time alone sorting out the domestic arrangements. My blogs changed accordingly; slightly domestic news one week, a description of an outing or an issue the second week; I thought of them as letters followed by stories. This is from the first letter, followed by the first story from Malawi.

Shifting base from South Africa to Malawi, at least for the next few years, has been quite a saga. I will not weigh you down with the excruciating details of departure which included such sadnesses as a final farewell to my much loved old dog, Goose, and to my trusty computer which grew legs and wandered off, as things do anywhere in Africa, while my back was turned.

I'll get to the topic of Malawi itself in a while. I haven't quite made up my mind about it yet. I think it's a bit like seeing a movie all your friends raved about, and when you finally see it you wonder why they were so delirious. Yes, it is pretty. Yes, the people are wonderful. Yes, the tourism tag "The Warm Heart of Africa" is very suitable... but... perhaps I just expected too much.

Zambia, on the other hand, I loved almost without reservation. Maybe this reluctance to embrace all things Malawian has to do with my living here. I spent months in Zambia as opposed to years, so I was effectively just passing through. Perhaps things look different from a permanent viewpoint? Stay with me as I explore the country and see what you think.

A home in Lilongwe
31st August

From the comfort of a friends flat we have been house-hunting, and have discovered a place that seems perfect to us. Plenty of space to spread ourselves indoors and a vast garden, mostly just lawn under wonderful indigenous trees. The site faces north at the end of a cul-de-sac in the heart of Lilongwe's diplomatic residences. The upper-crust suburban milieu is tempered by threadbare tarmac roads, patched and potholed, gardens the size of the average small-holding elsewhere, and open space given over to sweet-potato cultivation.

From the house our garden slopes down to the perimeter wall, giving us on the veranda—or kondi as it's called in the local Chichewa language—a lovely view of the little valley between us and the next group of houses, glimpsed through foliage surprisingly voluptuous for the end of the dry season. A small stream wanders through this marshy open area, and this is part of the fundamental policy that gives Lilongwe it's unique, if bewildering, layout and intangible atmosphere. It's a city that isn't.

The city is spread over a large hilly area and the natural drainage lines and seeps that run off the high ground are well wooded. These have been left undeveloped. Which means that even in the commercial centre of the city there is the feeling of being out in the bush.

For instance we saw long-crested eagle sitting on a street lamp a day or so ago—something you would never expect to see around the corner from the supermarket in most cities. And at night we quite often hear spotted hyena whooping it up as they stroll through the moonlit city centre. They are self-appointed, unpaid members of the city refuse collection department, and don't seem to suffer any lack. I've heard it rumoured that the occasional small dog will vanish in the night, but have yet to meet a bereft owner, so I'll reserve judgement. I assumed the scavengers were contained in the little local nature reserve, which is also smack in the centre of the capital, but it seems they have free range around the city through these remnant corridors of natural woodland.

The capital of Malawi, Lilongwe's city centre is about ten minutes out of town and has to be labelled "City Centre" or you would never know. This spacious layout, seemingly incorporating the extremely modern idea of wildlife corridors, makes it very difficult to get around if you don't have a motorcar. This includes the bulk of Malawians, since Malawi is about number seven in the ranks of the world's poorest countries. But it is very beautiful, with huge trees and glimpses of distant mountains between a sparse scatter of tall modern buildings.

Even flat life here is gracefully rural. I have yet to see a block of flats or the grim slab tenements like other cities have. There are rows of duplexes instead, and we are in one, just around the corner from the Capital Hotel. Sounds singularly unattractive, but the garden of this flat is perhaps a little larger than the one around my old house in Pretoria, and its trees tower way above the double story.

Even among the flats, the bird life is a delight. There was a golden oriole outside our window this morning, and yesterday I saw a yellow-bellied sunbird in the garden. A charming pair of pied wagtails bob and curtsy as we wander around admiring gardener Henderson's vigorous vegetables. Heuglin's robin is unfailingly vocal at dawn, and we have a resident squadron of pied crows who spend  their days tumbling about the sky, harassing the occasional yellow-billed kite, or stalking singly through the garden with an air of suppressed menace.

We took another trip out to the lake over the week-end. It's still strange to see river weed and fish eagle instead of sea-shells and sea-beasties. A huge water-boatman washed up, as long as my thumb, and we saw a sunbird's nest in in the crook of an agave flower-spike which hung over a busy pathway. The only note the bird took of passing traffic was to close  her beak every time someone walked under her. To our astonishment we seemed to be the only people who saw her or the nest. We are still not sure which sunbird it is, and of course our reference books are still in storage in Pretoria.

We'll be moving to our more permanent home within the next two weeks, and hopefully our luggage will join us soon after. I'm really looking forward to getting our own line connected to the new house and not having to trundle half-way round this most extended town to find a computer that is linked up. Roll on the advent of electronic independence!

September 1999

They say ice-hockey is the fastest game ever invented. I've seen one that is faster. It's called Try and Snatch my Breakfast and it's played between a fish-eagle and a team of five pied crows over Grand Beach on Lake Malawi.

Distracting your attention from the lake itself is quite deliberate, because it's something I haven't come to terms with yet. All that huge body of FRESH water! It's mind-boggling for an arid-region child like me. I had no trouble at all with the waves and the beach and the crash and splash and the absence of an opposite shore—it's all quite ordinary, in a new and beautiful way, as shore-lines are. But not to see shells on the beach was odd, and the absence of rock-pools full of sea anemones and star-fish was very disconcerting.

And the presence of water-weed like a shaggy carpet stitched below the Plimsoll line of boulders was positively unnerving.

I scrambled over granite boulders tumbled between sunset and the lake, listening to the hush and suck of waves. To my right the seeming sea, on the left a wooded granite koppie studded with baobabs and dassies. A fish eagle called and a pair of redwing starlings abseiled down a rock-face, searching out who knows what. Sitting quietly gazing across the teal-green wrinkled water, I saw the drab splattered rocks of Bird Island conjured into a sudden bright confection as it caught the last of the sun. Behind it florets of cumulous rose above the mist bank in a static tumble of glowing mother-of-pearl.

Quite entranced by the view I almost missed the fact that I was being watched too, and turned my head just in time to see a silky dark flank heel and slip under the water. The movement was so like a seal that I was confused again—are there freshwater seals? I know there are salt-water hippos in North Africa. Maybe it was a big fish?—but the sense of having been watched was so strong, and the movement so unfishlike that I didn't really believe that. Science himself smiled sweetly when he came rock-hopping back from his more agile explorations.

"Of course there are freshwater seals," he said, "They are called otters."

An otter! Not just ANY otter, but my first otter! We sat very still for a time in the futile hope that he'd come back for another look at us, but dusk came first and I had to make my way back before the dark left me fumbling hamfootedly.

Next morning I lazed on my back under a Natal mahogany listening to the waves, and watched the fish-eagle tease the crows. It really seemed deliberate. The bird had bagged itself a good big fish, but instead of sensibly flying to a convenient perch, in the accepted conservation-of-expensive-energy manner that we are told regulates the behaviour of all wild things, this bird seemed to set off on a victory lap. Was it chance that made it wander perilously close to a gang of aerobatic crows, brawling in one sector of the  sky? The eagle seemed to go deliberately out of its way to drag that tempting fish under the very tips of those ruffians' noses.

The resultant chase was highly entertaining for me, and I hope as much fun for the eagle, who shrugged off the combined onslaught with an almost off-hand dexterity. The crows were spectacular. They bombed and dived and glided and rolled and swooped and spun. The game had all the tension and breath-catching daring of a team of fighter-pilots in a dogfight. Naturally the fish-eagle was never really in any danger of losing his breakfast, but the crows certainly gave it all they had for a few minutes. There seemed to be a subtle final whistle, for the crows and the eagle gave up at the same moment, and sailed off to opposite ends of the sky, the eagle to perch out of sight, and the crows went back to aerial loitering.

St Georgess and the Dragonette
8th September

We moved into our new house over the weekend, and have had an interesting time pushing furniture about, trying to fathom the intricacies of the electrical system, exploring the nethermost regions of our garden (which my scientific advisor judges to be almost three-quarters of a hectare) and meeting the resident wildlife. Like the blue-headed tree agama, for instance.

This handsome fellow shares his time between scaling a tall large fruited bushwillow (*Combretum zeyheri*) and exploring the depth of the rainwater furrow below the veranda. He is about half a metre in length and is an Impressionists delight of pointillist spots—golden on his tail, lapis-lazuli on his nose. The two colours merge in an electric green up his broad neck and manage to invoke an impossible purple across his shoulders—I haven't got close enough to find out how he does that yet.

Another feature of the garden is what sounds like an entire established population of pearl-spotted owlets. These are the smallest of the raptors, diminutive bundles of buffy-pink and pearl-spotted feathers. They look adorable, all head and huge eyes, like babies do.

In compensation for their cutesy appearance they have a deeply ferocious nature. Napoleon had nothing on these guys. Their other distinction is an ear-splitting call which builds to an orgasmic crescendo and a series of irascible whistles which humans can only achieve through their teeth and with the full force of a large pair of male lungs. One of these owls seems to favour the tree just outside the guest bedroom, and our first visitor left this morning looking a tad shattered through lack of sleep.

He might have been even more shattered had he met the apparition that I encountered in the early hours of our first day in the new house.

I was quietly brewing a cup of tea when I turned to see a gigantic cockroach shamble through the door. This chap had to use the door, there being no crack big enough to accommodate him. He came staggering in, looking like he'd had a really rough night and was desperate for a good restorative breakfast. He eyed me speculatively. Being a modern maiden I refrained from calling upon a passing knight, and defeated the beast myself in single-shoed combat. My scientific advisor and I had an intense discussion over the corpse, which I could clearly see was a trophy specimen, but unimaginative Science, impressed though he was, refused to have it stuffed and mounted.

The domestic upheavals have not kept us from exploring a little of this lovely country, and next I'll introduce you to another little segment of it, but till then I've got to continue fighting my way through invisible constraints to get a telephone line to the house, and perhaps even one that works! Don't laugh, this is a magnum opus.

The good news is that our luggage is even now negotiating a passage through Botswana, and may reach us by the end of next week. Oh joy, access to my reference books is almost at hand.

Lake water lapping[5]
13th September

With Lake Malawi's Senga Bay less than two hours away, the lure is too great to resist. Driving out from Lilongwe, the coral trees are just breaking into crimson blossom. The scarlet flame creeper and soft bronze leaves of the miombo woodland herald spring among the winter-gold and burned black of the hillsides. Beyond them Malawi's mountains are a decorous misty blue.

These mountains amaze me. They fill the view, wild and varied like a bargain basement collection of sample mountain designs. "End of the Range" mountains, maybe. One is short and squat, the next is sharply alpine looking, another totters dizzily over a plunging ravine, the next is flat-topped, and yet another a tumbled heap of boulders. They look like the training ground for angels apprenticed to the Landscape Design department.

---

[5] I will arise and go now, for always night and day/I hear lake water lapping with low sounds by the shore;/While I stand on the roadway, or on the pavements grey,/I hear it in the deep heart's core.– W.B. Yeats

Our first visit to the lake was spent at the well-tended camping ground attached to the Livingstonia Hotel, nee the Grand Beach Hotel. On this second visit we turned off to the left just before the entrance to the hotel, and followed a little dirt road about a kilometre or two. The road ends at the door of the founding father of a conservation body called the Wildlife Action Group.

This is Georg Kloeble, tall, hollow-cheeked and energetic. He looks a bit like Jan Smuts, noble-nosed and goateed. Georg came to Malawi as a technician for a German electronics and communications company and got hooked. He fell in love with this delicate strip of Africa clinging to its voluptuous lake shore, and threw everything over to make a difference here.

Malawi, like most of Africa, has suffered the bewilderment of not being allowed to own her own land, and after generations of forgetting how it's done, is now confronted with the hopeless task of managing her own dwindling resources. The situation is compounded by a flood of enthusiastic foreign advisors who rush about making hope-stimulating sounds about sharing the resource cake between communities, tourism and wildlife. What nobody has the guts to say is that the wildlife is almost gone, and the beautiful Malawian forests are now perhaps only 40% of their former selves. The resource cupboard is just about bare. If this is the cake that is to be shared, there is nothing but crumbs with which to serve several hungry party-goers. In the case of the communities, the term 'hungry' is not used lightly.

Georg found a sympathetic partner in Malawi's Department of Forestry, who initiated conservation in Malawi. He has leased two of the department's assets, both suffering from a lack of financial resources. The first is this place on the lake shore, an old departmental guest house, tucked away among the boulders of a koppie just beyond the arm of Senga Bay. Overlooking a gentle scoop of lake called Leopard Bay, the house is destined to become a small retreat for lovers of wildlife and wilderness. So this is a preview of delights you might sample in six months or so.

I was fascinated by the variegated beach sand on Georg's tiny private beach. Shimmering powdery red and black and coarse gritty gold, the colours mingle together like an exotic tie-dye, and gleam purple in the spill and wash of gentle waves. I learned that this beach didn't just happen. Georg virtually created it.

Since the lake is a body of fresh water, the usual lakeside reeds grow easily, trapping silt and debris and creating their own compost which turns into good pond-type mud. Georg has chopped the reeds out and, shovelful by shovelful, sifted the flotsam and jetsam from the shoreline. He has carted way truckloads of rubbish, not just old smelly reeds and the odd dead fish, but tons of rusted tins, broken bottles and a mountain of discarded plastic, all the dross of modern so-called civilization.

With a handful of local assistants it's taken months of backbreaking work, but they have managed to coax back this little strip of tie-dyed magic, creating a tourist's delight and an irresistible invitation to bathe. Georg found me a paddle ski, and Science himself was literally roped into towing me out through the swell, around a spill of boulders to a tiny sheltered cove where we hoped to meet my elusive otter again.

We saw a cheeky group of dog-faced baboons chewing green mangoes, and a giant kingfisher, rust and charcoal like the lichen-splashed rocks. He dipped his head at us and traced a neat inverted parabola to an overhanging branch, a silent shadow against silent granite. Myriads of tiny glassy fish scattered from our splashing calves as we waded in to look at the beached carapace of a dugout canoe, long gone and semi-rotted, it's tattered hull patched and re-patched with oil cans, corrugated iron, and heavy duty plastic sheeting.

Later we sat under a cascade of sausage tree flowers (*Kigelia africana*), a living beaded curtain as elegant as an art nouveau stained-glass window. Crimson and lime-green, the flowers opened their softly scented throats to the evening air as we sipped frosted beer and watched the changing light make splendid the shabby stern of a water taxi, a local transport launch. This elderly craft plies a twice daily route between this little bay and Cape Maclear, a four hour journey rather longer than a trip directly across the lake, for here Lake Malawi is at its narrowest. Even so, the opposite shore is too far for sight.

Behind us a little troop of vervet monkeys are rattling leaves in a huge rock-breaker fig, and a fish-eagle yelps overhead. It's an evening of sensuous contentment.
Regarding Georg and his almost single-handed drive to rescue dwindling wildlife resources, his second project on the other Forestry asset I mentioned is a saga in its own right.

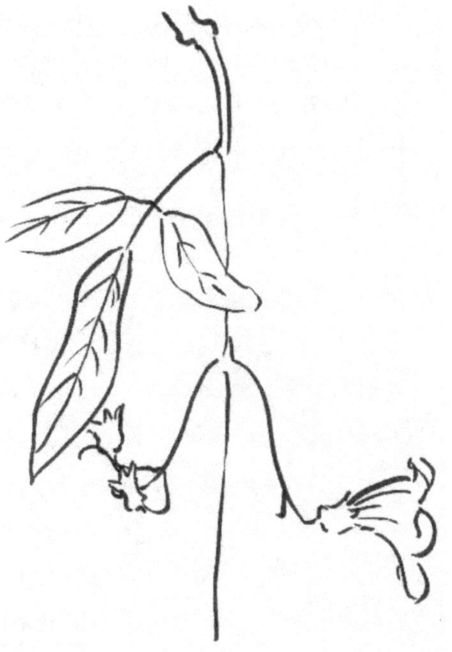

Mzuzu
15th September

Malawi seems to be the Heart of the Warmth... and it's not even summer yet! I'm told that this is an unusually cool moist winter, but by ten in the morning it's uncomfortably hot out. No doubt another aspect of Malawi that I will adjust to in time.

We've come up north to Mzuzu for various Wildlife Department workshops and meetings. Mountainous Mzuzu is famous for its coffee, which I'm told is particularly fragrant and flavourful. As a contented user of instant chicory powder, the delights of these subtleties are lost on me. The green and folded

little town, however, does have a certain charm. To my surprise, this being the dry end of a very dry winter, now is the flowering season. The streets are adorned with banks of plants, among them clouds of candy-pink begonias with reddish leaves and simple flowers carried on tall stalks.

I have never regarded begonias as a particularly good plant for landscaping purposes, in fact I privately agree with author Beverley Nichols who wrote, "Begonias are not flowers. They are a state of mind, and a very unpleasant one at that." These however are impressively exuberant.

Out among the plantations and tall brachystegia forest are little botanical wonderlands to discover, bright with yellows, purples, blues and cream. One of the more spectacular flowers is the spitting image of the purple tibushina—very like a plant we used to call lasiandra when it was a popular flowering shrub in urban Johannesburg in the 50s. They are both originally from South America, I think. This wild cousin has deep green velvet leaves, deeply veined and rimmed with red, and the five-petal flowers are a rich regal purple. I last saw this wild one in a sheltered groin of montaine forest on the Zoutpansberg near Louis Trichardt in South Africa. It took me years to find its name—*Dissotis princeps.*

Tuesday, we are told, our kit and kitundu will at last be here. All those reference books I thought I would have had by now are, we are reliably informed, at last actually on their way. I can't wait to get a look at Newman's Birds of Malawi, which I stupidly failed to bring with me.

Before that we'll visit a private forest reserve called Thuma a few kilometres south of the town of Selima, the only largish place between Lilongwe and Senga Bay on the Lake. Selima itself is notable for a really beautiful diminutive mosque, just two doors away from the "God Be With Us Garage And Service Station". Names are a delight here in Malawi. So far my favourite is one emblazoned on a building beside the road to Mzuzu. It proclaims the business housed there to be the "Money Comes Money Goes Investment Corporation."

Baobabs and Bamboo
20ᵗʰ September

Georg Kloeble, as I was saying in the "lake water lapping" story, is waging a small private war against the decimation of Malawi's natural resources.

Since any war is expensive, and conservation is especially so, Georg foresaw that he would soon run out of money. So he did two things. He leased and is revamping the Forestry Rest House at Leopard Bay as a source of income, and he launched a non-government conservation organisation in his homeland Germany to raise funds. This is the Wildlife Action Group, which organises working holidays in Malawi for European science students and enthusiasts. These pay a fairly low fee to cover their very rustic board and lodging and are provided the opportunity of working on research projects in Africa—in Georg's private conservation area. In effect he has created a fund-raising organisation which gets people to pay him for working for him. It's very clever, and a small insight into the Kloeble mind-set and methodology.

But let me introduce you to the specific patch of Malawi that Georg has taken under his wing. It's an area of natural forest to the west of Salima called the Thuma Forest Reserve (and like most African names, the t and the h are pronounced as two separate sounds.)

Thuma was proclaimed a forest reserve back in the early 20s. Since then, growing poverty has taken its toll and protection of the area has gradually given way to increased harvesting of wood for fires and building, and extensive poaching of the now almost extinct wildlife.

Thuma is reminiscent of a volcanic crater, with a ring of protective hills enclosing a sublime bit of African old-wood forest. For someone from a more arid region like myself, the size of the trees is a constant surprise. Sometimes so surprising that I fail to recognise a familiar friend because it's just so much bigger than I've ever seen it before. And the juxtaposition of the familiar with the foreign is fascinating.

Take the baobabs for instance. Probably because of their succulent-like appearance I think of them as essentially low-land arid-zone trees, associated with bald rocks and dry heat. Yet here they are, thriving on this sometimes steeply rising ground, often cheek by jowl with indigenous bamboo! To me, bamboo is stuff found in high rainfall areas, jungle plants dependent on humidity. Useless to look them up in the tree book, since they are actually a member of the grass family. Bamboo relatives are running wild in Thuma. Like so many areas where wildlife has taken a beating, there is little left to keep rampant grass in check. The lack of elephants and buffaloes is especially noticeable, since they tend to munch down a fair bit and trample even more, leaving the more easily eaten game, like zebra and wildebeest, a clear view which encourages them to venture into the open and chew down the grass even more.

To Georg's delight he has seen the tracks of both buffaloes and elephants in the past few months, sure indications that Thuma is recovering. The steps he's taken over three years to achieve this are unusual, sometimes controversial, and occasionally brilliant.

For example, because of the constant threat of poaching, Georg felt that to accustom the wildlife to the presence of his hand-picked game guards would encourage a possibly lethal trust of humans in general. Yet, tourists won't pay to see only the fleeing rump of a startled animal, and the eventual goal for Thuma is to be a fully productive (and profitable) haunt for tourists as well as wildlife.

Georg has a unique solution to the problem. He sprays his guards, himself and any legitimately visiting vehicle or person with a secret, highly distinctive, scent. He mixes the perfume himself and the formula is closely guarded. The animals are learning that this specific aroma is non-threatening, but maintain their wariness of anyone or anything else. Such a simple solution to a complex problem is almost genius.

Some of Georg's management techniques are remarkably high-tech in this third world and undeveloped area. For instance, his game guards work with a global positioning system (GPS) which provides co-ordinates for their daily reports[6]. These are radioed

---

[6] Bear in mind that this was written seventeen years ago, when cell phones were not much smaller than the hand-sets of land-line telephones, and just two years

to Georg at Salima who picks them up through his computer which automatically charts the GPS readings attached to the guards reports. If the GPS reading doesn't coincide with the report, Georg knows immediately that the guard has not done the patrol as reported.

As well as providing a safe haven for wildlife, the vegetation at Thuma is protected. Illegal and uncontrolled wood chopping has been stopped and a quota system developed for resources like the much prized and extremely useful bamboo poles. Far from feeling alienated, the communities on the borders of the reserve have come to see Georg as an authority to whom they can turn for assistance. When the government suddenly put up the price of bamboo poles by more than 500%, Georg was the man they appealed to, to approach the government on their behalf.

Some of Georg's conservation methods are domineering, authoritarian or para-military and politically unacceptable to many. He would certainly not be able to practise his kind of conservation in any official government or foreign-aid-funded project. But as a private person, funded by an NGO he himself initiated, he is free to run his project as he sees best.

And with visible signs of success. Good for Georg Kloeble. His efforts show the benefit of a creative man with initiative acting freely. It's not a method that

---

after Nokia brought out the first full keyboard for text messages in the USA. The idea of a personal GPS system was absolutely astonishing, and to find one in operation in rural south-central Africa even more so.

would work universally, or even an example to follow in detail. But what is inspirational is how much one man with energy and imagination can achieve when poverty and apathy has stalled any conservation ethic.

Post script, 2016. Georg's revamped forestry guest house is called Safari Lodge, near Salima. Trip Advisor shows it to be a little more manicured than when we were there, but still with its day visitors of monkeys and dassies and the eternal beautiful views out over Lake Malawi.

Peeved in paradise
22ⁿᵈ September

I remember being told a little apocryphal story about an American who couldn't understand why there was no African equivalent of the term 'mañana'. The question was asked of an inhabitant with a wealth of African experience, who gave the problem deep thought before replying,

"Actually, there are plenty of terms with roughly the same meaning, but none that have that sense of urgency."

Painfully true. But everything in life has a price. If I have to pay for having one foot in the bush by gritting my teeth about delays, disappointments and general dysfunctionality, I can hardly complain. And until I'm used to it, hopefully people will mistake the tightened lips and set teeth for a grin.

I'm irked mostly about the consistent non-arrival of our kit, though the non-arrival of a telephone line and various other little annoyances play a part too. But the most infuriating is the absence of everyday essentials that I fully expected to have almost a month ago. I'm suffering such serious sense of humour failure on this score that if my kitundu doesn't pitch up on Friday—which is the most recently promised e.t.a—I might even resort to telling you which international removals/transport company is responsible for my frustration.

However, it's hard to stay peeved for long in this place. The imperceptible swing towards summer is tinting the air with a million subtle perfumes as the acacias and the dombeyas come into flower. The sky is a deep intense blue and a mist of new leaves hangs like a thin green veil over smoke-grey branches. The miombo woodlands' new leaves are giving their impression of a Canadian autumn—all copper and bronze and rose. As the days lengthen these will mature to deep rich green. In Liwonde National Park there are random masses of the *adenia* flower called impala lily or Sabi star depending on where you hail from.

A trip to Zambia's South Luangwa National Park was very satisfying—but I'm going to save that for another time, when I'm less slit-eyed about a particular truck snailing it's interminable way through that country. My books, my books, a kingdom for my books!

Liwonde National Park
27th September

If you look at a map of Malawi, you will see the lake slither down the eastern edge of the country looking very much like a diving, legless sea-beastie with jaws agape. Dangling from the tip of its nose by a thread is bite-sized Lake Malombe. The thread happens to be the Shire (pr. Shear-ree) River, the single watercourse that drains the second deepest of Africa's great lakes.

Liwonde National Park runs alongside, sometimes straddling, the Shire as it flows between Lake Malombe and the little town of Liwonde on its headlong rush to meet the Zambezi. The Park has a number of specialties that make it noteworthy, like Lillian's lovebird, which is not found anywhere else in Malawi, and the rare red flowered euphorbia *(Euphorbia lividiflora)*.

The lovebirds I certainly saw on this first brief visit. Not well enough to satisfy my curiosity though. These little feathered gems flash by like enamelled bullets. You'll hear the unmistakable lovebird shriek, and a small group will screech past, giving just enough of a glimpse to show they are lovebirds and vanish into the elegant gallery of mopani trees. I saw three or four groups without once managing to get a glimpse of their heads.

Liwonde is more than noteworthy in my book. It is restrainedly beautiful, reminiscent of Gorongoza on a small scale, with modest floodplains and festive palms. The three hills that give this flat area definition are speckled with evenly strewn black rocks and lightly wooded with combretums, commiferas and the softly gleaming ghostly trunk of the occasional large leafed star chestnut tree *(Sterculia quinqueloba)*.

For me, one of the delights was an offshoot of the scarcity of game. Liwonde, like all of Malawi's parks, has suffered terribly from simple poverty and poaching for the pot, as well as the really despicable organised poaching that happens in any impoverished country. This is not to say that there is no game in Liwonde—compared to Gorongoza, the place is fairly rampant with wildlife. Elephants and hippos are plentiful. We also saw waterbuck, impala, bushbuck and kudu—but not in the sort of numbers one could expect in the 538 square kilometres that comprises the Park.

One of the results of this scarcity is that the plant called *Adenium obesum*, the Sabi star or impala lily, has not been browsed down to the stubby shrub found further south. In Liwonde the plants are up to two metres in height and in August were a mass of blooms. They are rather like miniature baobabs. Obesum indeed. The star-shaped flowers appear on the podgy grey stems like a minor miracle, white or pink with a crinkley crimson or shocking pink border, and here they were in such profusion that the display seemed touchingly extravagant, like the flowers at Princess Di's funeral.

The Shire River and its abundance of water-birds (Liwonde Park boasts 410 bird species—about two thirds of the checklist for the whole of Malawi) is another pleasure, but I'll tell you all about that when I've had more than a fleeting introductory visit and can give you an in-depth picture. With any luck, that could be quite soon.

AAAAAAAaaaaaaaaaaah!
30ᵗʰ September

At last! Here I am in this beautiful country, not only relishing all the new experiences of Malawi, but ALSO with my old accustomed things around me! Talk about the best of both worlds!

The down side is that now that I've got all my stuff I just want to play with it. It feels like playing housey-housey when I was a kid. I want to make things on the sewing machine, and slop a bit of paint around, and revel in all those beautiful books I haven't seen in months. I want to bake biscuits and make old fashioned pots full of tea (in a cup! on a tray!) to drink while I browse through these old friends like Roberts' Birds and Smithers' Mammals. I want to hang

paintings on the walls and swap the curtains around
yet again. I don't want to do anything else.
Write? Who wants to write?
I'm off to bake a second batch of biscuits.

The ART of resource management
4th October

If you thought the link between art and wildlife conservation was restricted to painted portraits of lordly and elegant creatures to nail to a wall like a civilised trophy, or impressionistic landscape views like an imitation window, think again. Not just "fine art", but ART *and* the performing arts.

To begin at the beginning. ART stands for the Africa Resources Trust. As its name implies it came into being to promote sustainable use of natural resources. That begins to sound like agency-speak, but what it means is simply sensible conservation and land use. The aim is to give rural people the knowledge and the opportunity to manage the assets provided them by nature—such as thatching grass, medicinal herbs, clay for brick making, wood for cooking fires and building, fibre for basket making, impala to eat, and so on.

Here comes the part that I find fascinating. One of the huge problems with an initiative like this is that it is highly fashionable and popular with aid agencies, who employ teeming herds of sociologists and ecological accountants and economists and gender specialists to hive around drawing impressive salaries and talking abstract idealism to each other in a happy congratulatory way. Or sadly consolatory, depending on the situation.

I'm being overly belittling and dismissive. In fact they are all extremely well intentioned and sincerely wish to save wildlife, the environment, and, mostly, the people who are utterly dependent on untamed nature for survival.

The problem is that the field of Community Based Natural Resource Management is a western intellectual exercise. It has embraced terms that flow impressively off the tongue with seemingly little effort, like "CBNRM", "governance processes", "capacity development", "inequitable access" and even more basic "sustainability" and "resource management". These are terms with so many syllables that even the average well educated townie would have difficulty knowing off the cuff what these chaps are talking about. How much do you suppose a rural subsistence farmer, possibly illiterate and with English as a second language if at all, will understand?

Well now, here comes genius to the rescue. ART realised that the major problem is translating these high-flown thoughts into the practical nitty-gritty that a farmer can lay her hands on. Or his, of course. And an interesting symbiotic relationship was generated. A fascinating marriage of opposites. Science and theatre.

So it was that I was privileged to accompany a pair of ART sociologists to Liwonde National Park as they set about delving into the problems that face communities living on the boundary of the Park. This basic information is processed by ART into a list of issues that need to be addressed by both the Park and the neighbouring communities. It's the skeleton of a scenario which is passed on to a group of actors called Theatre for Africa who give it life and breath, and a play is born.

Theatre for Africa is well known internationally for stunning work on nature and wildlife issues, focussing on the human drama implicit in them. Their plays are superbly judged; full of movement, tension, humour, music and joyful illusion. If half the traditional stage-bound companies had as much skill and daring, theatre would eclipse television in popularity.

The group, led by Nicholas Ellenbogen, are as dedicated to the environment as they are to the art of theatre. Each performance by these superlative actors serves a double purpose. It entertains primarily, but it also highlights problems and enacts possible solutions. In acting out an example of a problem even the most intellectual concept becomes easily digestible. The same play can bring dawning realisation to unsophisticated rural people and an equally vital dawning realisation to moneyed consumers in New York, Geneva or London.

What will happen now that the fundamental issues are identified, is that two seasoned Malawian actors will be taken to Cape Town for several months of intensive training. They will return to the little town of Liwonde with a play to perform for the community and National Park officials. And for the tourists at Mvu Lodge too, since being an actor also provides a means of earning a living. Aside from facilitating change through establishing a sound understanding of the problem, this embryonic theatre company will pass on to other potential thespians in the village their acquired skills, not the least important of which is the ability to take a common problem and turn it into a play.

Well done Theatre for Africa, and well done ART. Long may the union last.

Lilongwe, and loving it
6th October

I'm still revelling in getting re-acquainted with all my old stuff. Especially moving has been the almost tearful moment of restoration of my push-bike to my anxious arms—not to mention my equally anxious legs. The anxiety of the latter was considerably more profound since it's only by means of a bicycle that one discovers exactly how unflat this charming city is.

Believe me, it is deeply unflat. My unfit calves quail at the thought of another bout of exploration, but the benefit of cycling (for me particularly) is that I can watch the scenery instead of my feet most of the time, and I only periodically hit the odd rock or pothole and pitch off. I can get further on the bike than I ever possibly could on my one-and-a-half feet, and the sense of expanded horizons is delectable.

Right now is a wonderful time for getting out into the soft air. The combretums are in full flower. I don't think I ever noticed them blooming before, since the flowers are very small, greenish yellow and quite high up. I probably just understood the mist of young green to be new leaves. But we have one flowering right next to our raised veranda, and it fills the air with a soft romantic perfume and the dizzy sound of mumbling bees. Little prinias, batises, sunbirds and canaries flirt and fidget among the flowers.

Cycling up and down (I don't know how it's done, but this part of Lilongwe definitely has more ups than downs) these quiet suburban streets fills the lungs with the almost rural smells of early bushveld spring, and the eyes and ears feast on the Malawi peculiarities—the continually (frustratingly) hidden bird with a call like a squeaky wheel slowing down. It goes: "whip.whip..whip...wheep...wheeep... wheeeep..... whoooop .... woooooop" and grinds to a depressed halt. Nobody I've asked can tell me what this squeaky-wheel bird is. They tend to look at me a little oddly though.

But I have recognised another of the speciality birds around here—Schalow's lourie (or turaco). It  looks very like Livingstone's lourie, which is a dead ringer for the Knysna lourie, except for the length of its crest. Schalow's has gone completely over the top, as fashion freaks will, by having a crest so long it curls forward when fully erect, and streams behind in flight giving the bird a strange pre-historical outline, like a technicolour pterodactyl. With Cleopatra eye-liner.

They are unbelievably gorgeous. Somehow those deep garnet-red wings are always a surprise. Such an exotic feeling having them hop through garden trees as if this were still forest.

Livingstone—David, I presume—features quite strongly here (we spotted Livingstone's flycatcher feeding among acacia flowers this afternoon) perhaps a relic of the flood of Scots missionaries who came in after his death—in his wake, to coin a phrase. I've not been as aware of his sombre pig-headed presence as much elsewhere in Africa. Hopefully I'll make it up to Livingstonia before too long, and bring back an account of Malawi's earliest mission station there.

But if things really go as I plan, I'll be swanning off to Kasungu National Park around Tuesday. It's 180 kilometres north-west of Lilongwe, and needless to say, I'm looking forward to it hugely.

Dedza
11th October

Less than an hour's drive from Lilongwe on the Blantyre road is Dedza Mountain, with a little village of the same name sprawled at its foot. Once a thriving forestry station, the village has shrunk until all that remains is a scattering of small businesses, a saw mill just ticking over, a golf course and a large and flourishing pottery.

To the inhabitants of Lilongwe, this last is the main reason for a trip out to Dedza, since the pottery also runs a rather nice coffee shop. Most people will tell you that driving out to Dedza is a very pleasant way to spend a lazy Saturday afternoon, but for a few, Dedza is an irresistible weekend destination. Not the village, the mountain.

Rising over 2 000 metres, Dedza has a gentle look about it. Much of the mountain is afforested, its benign sides cloaked in plantations of pine and the occasional patch of fir trees. But if you keep on up the rather steep but still passable road, you emerge above the pines and find yourself in a magnificent area, a patchwork of high grasslands and dense montane forest. It's glorious.

We spent a rather chilly weekend camping up there late in August. It's a forest reserve, and I believe there is a forest rest-house up there somewhere, but we took our trusty tent along, and pitched it in a sheltered bend in the old forestry road. I had not given a thought to the altitude, and the cold caught me utterly by surprise. Next time I will be hung about with woollies, and better able to enjoy the spectacular views.

We walked up to the summit, me nursing the half-foot by going backwards up steep parts or resorting to hands and knees, a primitive four-wheel-drive mode that is wonderfully effective. If I can make the summit, just about anyone can. From there one scans a dizzying full circle of misty distant Malawi, hazy blue and hilly. Here and there the mist thickens to the milk-white plume of a veld fire. Directly east of us Lake Malawi pulled the cocoon of haze closer and refused to show her face.

Looking down from high wilderness reminds me of gazing into rich tidal pools. In shifting cloud shadow and diffuse sungleam I almost expect to see the darting shape of a fish glint silver over a distant hummock of land.

Teeth clamped against the bracing cold, I examined the crop of graffiti the summit has acquired. It is unlike any other "Joe was here" graffiti I've seen. For a start, it's all fairly small, and almost without exception, neatly written in clear capitals. The next surprise it that all the names are Malawian. More than a brag of conquest, these neat painted inscriptions have a subdued respectful quality, and seem to be almost a mark of pilgrimage for the lovelorn local.

It's an interesting phenomenon. The western perception of aesthetics is very different to the African, and there seem to be relatively few African outdoor enthusiasts. Yet here, on the very top of Dedza, is a record of hords of Malawian hikers, to whom being at this lovely high point has meant something special. They have marked their presence with so much restraint that they shame our Western hooligan cousins who cannot see the dignity of stone.

Scrambling and slithering my way down again, a coven of white necked ravens gathered to discuss my progress. Tattered as old umbrellas they seemed mockingly malicious, like Shakespeare's weird sisters in the Scottish play. At the base of the rocky summit a shy black-fronted bushshrike, masked like a miniature

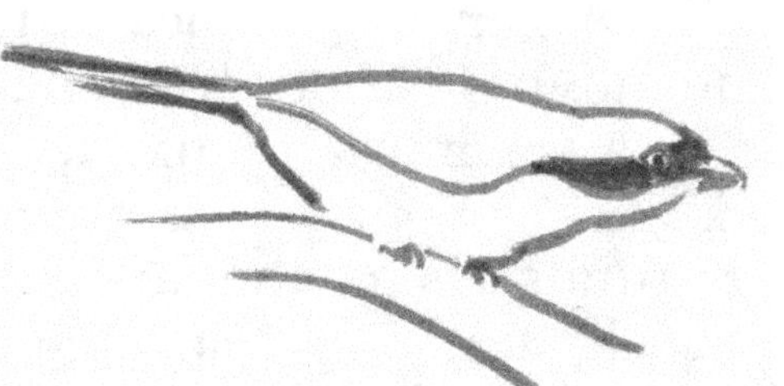

bandit but with breast cheerfully ablaze with sunset orange, came clear out of the bush to cock a little red eye at me.

Generally the birds were extremely frustrating. The pockets of forest are so dense. All that can be seen is a sudden flurry of wings if you're lucky, mostly it's just the call that reaches you on the grassland, a constant ringing foreign sound that it impossible to identify without at least a glimpse of size or feathers.

The plants were less retiring. The whole mountain seemed in the throes of a botanical festival.

The pink dombeya (*Dombeya burgessiae*) was one of the few I recognized, its massed banks of showy rose-pink blooms punctuated by the rich mauve and purple pea-like flowers of at least two varieties of polygala, and lilac scented fronds of what looked like sagewood (*Buddleja salviifolia*). These were offset by an extravagance of yellow daisies and serried ranks of blue trumpets from voluptuously flowering herb bushes as tall as a logger. Delicately scented, these flower spikes were armed with thousands of little glue-beaded hairs, which seemed to effectively trap any likely looking pollinator. Puzzling behaviour in a plant that is hanging out all the flags for procreation.

I also found a beautiful specimen of the small-leafed dragon tree, a member of the Yucca family, looking very like an overgrown escapee from someone's pot-plant collection, and a small clump of ensete, the indigenous wild bananas with beautiful pink-veined leaves and bunches of leathery fruits like imitation bananas filled, in a botanical prank, with hard pips. Doreen Bolnick, in her book on common wild flowers of the area, reminds one of the fact that bananas are not trees at all, but large succulent perennial herbs. Amazing stuff. It's a bewildering mixture of delight and frustration, being in a new country; so many things are unusual and exciting, and it's so difficult to find out what it is you're looking at. I look forward to getting familiar, in time, with Dedza's riches.

Strawberry City
13th October

Malawi has been doing the most extraordinary thing with the weather in the last week. It's October, traditionally called Suicide Month in these parts, since it literally gets too hot for some people to handle. At least that's what I'm told.

Yet for the last five days or so it's felt like autumn. Damp and blustery weather, with a mean and sneaky chill in the air. Even the early morning mist of wood smoke, hanging in the hollow of the dambo beyond our garden wall, is reminiscent of autumn. Quite sad, actually, for those who planned to do a veld-managing bush-encroachment-discouraging hot burn in mid-October; with the cold nights and clammy air, the grass seems reluctant to burn. What should be raging veld fires are patchy little half-hearted affairs, shy to begin and easily intimidated.

Not that I'm complaining about the coolth I'll have you know. It's been almost welcome. I'll admit that camping in the teeth of what felt like an arctic blast in Kasungu National Park last week was interesting. The second night we decided that any fool could be uncomfortable and headed for the shelter and comparative warmth of the grass chalets at Lufupa Camp. It was almost as cold as camping on Dedza

Mountain. Next week you can read about the Kasunga trip, with some dark questions about a South African game capture operation there.

This cold snap has caused a logjam in my culinary production line. I'd been churning out a range of hot-weather coolers from chilled soup to fruit ices. Picture us ploughing our way grimly through them all, dressed in an extra layer of woollies.

One of the most successful of my ill-timed sorties into the mysteries of thermo-regulatory cuisine is a chilled cucumber and strawberry soup. Sheer lip-smacking delight, I tell you, and worth dragging on an extra pair of socks for. This recipe comes out of a book by Roald and Felicity Dahl, *Memories with Food at Gypsy House* and I was really pleased to find something different to do with the strawberries.

Lilongwe must be the strawberry capital of Malawi. Every street has three or four vendors of the glistening fruit. These heart shaped and fragrant vegetable rubies are wonderfully flavourful—straight from the green stems I suspect, not via the cooling rooms, or irradiating plants or whatever indignities modern city demands place on them. We are all eating strawberries until they come out of our ears, strawberry cake, strawberry milkshakes, strawberry ice-cream, strawberry mousse...

And now—strawberry soup! Thank you, Roald Dahl!

Kasungu
18th October

Malawi lies beside the lake like a fat shadow, as though the lake is miles above the land and the shadow sprawls below, bigger and not very exact. Smack in the middle and just above the broadest part of this shadow-land sit the twin game reserves of Kasungu and Nkhota-kota, the first hugging the border with Zambia, the second closer to the lakeside.

They are often spoken of in one breath, as if they lie together and are one unit. In fact they are about 100 kilometres apart and are vastly different. Where Kasungu National Park is on the flat central African plateau and is almost wall to wall *Brachystegia* woodland, Nkhota-kota Wildlife Reserve is on the escarpment, wild hilly country with the odd high patch of ancient thick montane forest.

Most of my time was spent at Kasungu, which at first glance could be called uninspiring—the vistas of *Brachystegia*, despite the grace of the trees themselves and their spectacular spring colouring, appear monotonous. This is the sort of landscape that would invoke a stifled yawn from dedicated townies, and even the bush-baptised can find it a little irritating.

Brachystegia woodland is notoriously bad game viewing country. There is just too much cover, and those animals that enjoy the woodlands know how to use them to best effect, and are very hard to see.

Nevertheless we were rewarded with a number of surprising sightings that made the trip exceptional. Here and there the woodland gives way to a dambo, a vlei area of marshy grassland, and these are wonderful spotting grounds. The first surprise was an oribi, a gazelle-like dwarf antelope, a reddish-gold creature with a distinctive white rump and black tufted tail. Curiosity not only killed the cat, but it has done the oribi a severe disservice

too. Their inquisitiveness has made them an easy target for hunters, so it's quite a thrill to see one.

Soon afterwards a tubby little Sharpe's grysbok, even smaller than the oribi, barrelled away through the grass like an overgrown rabbit, its fat brown haunches bunched and bobbing. This was a first for me, and though the glimpse was fleeting, it was a delight to meet this knee-high antelope.

And within a few minutes there was the cob-type antelope, the reedbuck, statue-still against the fringe of forest around the dambo. Medium-sized and graceful, its corrugated horns form gentle crescents above the alert head, rather like a miniature waterbuck. Again, this was a first for me.

But the greatest thrill of all was to spot a leopard, frozen in mid-prowl across a dambo near Dwangwa Camp in the north, the long elegant back dappled with its own sunlight in the shade of tall trees. She stayed immobile, staring yellowly at us across the grass heads,  then brought her hindquarters under her in a fluid movement to assume the classic feline pose of serene unconcern. But she never took her eyes off us. A few timeless minutes later she tucked her head down and slinked off through the glade to vanish into the tall grass beyond. The grace of her stayed with us for the rest of the day, like a special benison.

It was as well, for in truth the marked scarcity of game is very noticeable. In discussing this with the research scientists in the park, a disturbing if vague story came to light. It seems that recently a South African game capture team was at Kasungu, removing buffalo, zebra, Lichtenstein's hartebeest, eland and roan, to translocate to Liwonde National Park in the south. Reports from different sources give differing opinions on the numbers proposed and taken, so the facts are confused and garbled. But there are disturbing questions that should be asked.

For a start, why take game from a park that is patently already under-stocked, simply to move it to another park? Robbing Peter to pay Paul has never been sound practice. There appears to have been no survey done to establish numbers before the translocation, and there are rumours that in the case of eland or Lichtenstein's hartebeest almost double the agreed quota was taken. Why?

I'm concerned about the roan antelope particularly, since they are known to be difficult to move. It is said that there were five or six mortalities, which is to be expected with these sensitive creatures. But is it acceptable, when roan are already on the endangered list?

And why was this operation done close to the only tourist lodge in Kasungu? The few remaining head of game are now so skittish that any kind viewing is almost impossible.

My own lasting impression of Kasungu was the most surprising sighting of all. One zebra. A single zebra. I don't think I've ever seen just one zebra. It stood still for a nervous second, then wheeled away and galloped out of sight.

Nostalgia
19th October

Hello nostalgically from Lilongwe

Which is not to say longingly—just harking back with a soft little smile, I'm sure you know the feeling. The trigger that launched me into this mood of mini-retrospection was old One-eye, the elderly computer that trundled up with our goods from South Africa.

This rather doddery piece of equipment seems to have had its brain scrambled by the move. I sympathise entirely, transplanting old-wood is never easy, especially for the plant—but among the jetsam of a sinking electronic intellect I discovered the last piece I wrote in Pretoria before the move to Malawi.

It brought back vividly the whole ambiance of my Pretoria base, my bay-windowed study/studio that started life as the garage; the bird-table that the black collared barbets seemed to think was their exclusive property, my disarmingly ugly wire-haired dachshunds who ate more birds than it is decent to contemplate let alone record, including most of those same barbets and a sulphur-crested cockatoo my son's girlfriend was hand-rearing.

We are dogless here in Lilongwe, a state the birds in this garden will unconsciously benefit from no doubt. It's an unusual state for a Lilongwean, residents have at least two, sometimes as many as five. The big gardens can handle the canine traffic, and most people feel it is a security essential. The dogs are peculiarly impressive for two reasons, one visual, the other auditory.

The visual aspect is a health precaution. The dogs require constant dipping against fleas, ticks and I think some kind of biting fly, and this service is provided by the vet in Old City. Gardeners or kitchen-hands gather up the leads in a bunch, and walk the generally dust-coloured dogs all the way down to old town, and back again. On the way back they are damp and dust-coloured.

The other peculiarity of Lilongwe dogs is that they don't seem to bark. In Pretoria the dogs were ardent barkers, keeping at it most of the day. Nerve wracking if you worked from home. In Lilongwe they are almost universally silent during the day. They save their energy for later.

Once it's really dark, and lights in bedroom windows wink out, the dogs come into their own. Chins lifted and eyes narrowed, the concert begins. Great operatic canine choirs echo and re-echo across the roof-tops and roll mournfully up the wooded seep-lines. It's astounding what variety can be achieved by several dedicated dogs. I have no idea why they don't bark, but it's simply not the done thing for watchdogs here. They howl. I wonder if they learned it from the resident hyenas?

Come to think of it, I haven't heard the hyenas since we moved a little further from the City Centre.

That says something interesting about Lilongwe, but I'm not quite sure what.

The sound of one hand chopping
25th October

Hello from the wooden Heart of Africa.

Last night I sat in the garden to watch the full moon rise over Malawi. Rich as a sun-ripened mango, it glowed between a tracery of branches against the dove-feather breast of evening. A silken breeze whispered through young leaves, and even the mosquitoes were considerate in their abstinence.

There are times when the sheer beauty of this country makes the eyes sting. There is a background of infinite sadness behind this grace, it's not just me being sentimental. It's so sad and inevitable that it almost feels psychotic.

Malawi lives on trees. Once blanketed in miombo and montane woodland, hard times have taken their toll. The blanket is moth-eaten and threadbare. The landscape between Lilongwe and the Lake is nibbled down to the nub, a rolling vista of scrub scattered with mango trees and the occasional tortured relic of a forest giant, limbs being gradually amputated until the mangled trunk itself succumbs.

Wood is Malawi's life blood. It is used for hearth fires, for warmth and cooking, for lighting in a country where electricity is still predominantly a rare privilege. It is used in building as roof supports, doors and window frames; for furniture and dug-out canoes; for household implements and generating cash income through carvings for tourists. And when a house is built of baked bricks, wood is used to fire the kilns.

It is said that when Malawi's posh capital Lilongwe was built, the bricks required for the project denuded the area of trees for a 150 kilometres along access roads around the city. Today if you look over Lilongwe and its surrounds, the only forest area is within the suburbs—the usual garden afforestation of indigenous trees and planted exotics. And the thin remnant woodlands in the marshes and streams through the city.

In an effort to ease the pressure, woodlots of the Indian tree Gmelina were planted and seem to flourish. The big snag is that one has to pay for the privilege of cutting the wood. Hard when you're broke. If you sneak off into the marshes, you can fell a tree or two at no cost whatsoever. So the tree cover along the streams get thinner and thinner, and privileged, affluent residents like myself get painfully sensitised to the sound of an axe.

If a visitor can see the degradation so easily, why have the Malawians done nothing about it? The answer is simple. All of Africa knows that life is tough. Survival is hard won and never assured. Sometimes you make it, sometimes you don't. Death is inevitable. There is no point in kicking against the pricks; take what you can while you can, for tomorrow is in the lap of the gods. And when the trees are gone, then the trees are gone. They are not gone yet, so why discuss it?

Yes, life is hard, life is about survival. And the beauty of a full moon is that it allows more time for chopping wood.

There now—instead of a letter, I've written an essay. It's just that I do feel very strongly about this problem, and as I write there is the sound of chopping coming in through my study window. Malawi is the seventh poorest country in the world. Protecting trees for their aesthetic value is not pro-survival for the average family.

Malawi is not alone in this. I was once told by a British ecologist of a conversation he had with a Welsh farmer, who justified his apparently wanton destruction of old-wood by saying, in the sweetly melodious Welsh accent, "As you know, trees are useless, unsightly things, and sheep hide behind them!" Till next week, try not to chop any trees down.

November 1999

Waiting for the rains
1st November

It's another still evening in this corner of the Warm Heart.

The Malawi sky is pale as agate and a dry breeze fidgets tender spring leaves. The grass is winter blond in the dambo below the house, and a bumble bee drones against the window pane, trying to reach the cooling air outside.

Me too. I feel like I need to rush out there and let the slow darkness cool my skin, brave the first crop of early mosquitoes for the sake of coolth. In an hour or so the moon will rise, a crescent of molten magma serenaded by crickets. Better to be outside with the insects than droning away against the hot eye of the monitor in this airless study. My ears thirst for the sound of frogs.

All of Malawi is in a subdued state of waiting. Everything is covered with a fine layer of dust and drifting carbon scraps from veld fires. Beyond our garden wall the dry grass is being turned into neat rows of hoed earth, a patchwork of corrugations like a corduroy quilt. The sound of chopping has momentarily given way to the sound of badza's biting the dry earth. Patches of overgrown weeds are fired, shrubs hacked back, and the neat expectant furrows grow under bent heads and glistening backs.

In Lilongwe city centre the streets are being repaired. Or prepared, I'm not sure which. It's the first time I've seen tarmac-surfaced roads being graded. Not the entire road, just the dirt shoulder. There is much scattering of additional sand and grading and sweeping. Getting it all ship-shape before the rains come and devastate the edges again.

Even the crows will be pleased to see the rain. The one that has patrolling rights on our garden will

be particularly pleased. He and I are getting fairly mutually fed up about the bird bath. It was put in quite recently, and within a matter of hours the crow had found it. I was initially delighted. I was quite sure his splashing would draw the other birds. Hah! Not this crow!

The crow who shared our garden at the flat was naive enough to think we might be worth training. His determined effort to teach us to throw him scraps had a certain innocent charm about it. This crow saw at once that we would not be worth training and has ignored us studiously. His snubbing has a flavour of cynicism about it that I find slightly offensive. But he was instantly captivated by the birdbath, and I fell for his enthusiasm. He'd be there at odd time throughout the day, dabbling about, sometimes only for a moment, sometimes he stayed for quite a while.

Then I started to find the oddest things in the birdbath. The centipede I could explain, and perhaps the gardener had rinsed his lunch plate under the tap to leave what looked like bits of corn porridge. But a chop bone? It took a while for the truth to dawn on me. Old crow is soaking his food in my birdbath! Yesterday I found the seriously second-hand corpse of a tree-agama belly-up at the bottom. Gross!

When I complained to my scientific adviser, he remarked that the crow was probably old and short of teeth. That would explain the need to soak his food, but it also highlights the fact that blindly accepting statements from a scientist can be fraught with hazards.

So the crow and I are at daggers drawn. I hurl abuse at him and he eyes me evilly and wishes acidly that I would mind my own business. We both wish the rains would come.

Mua than expected
4th November

From Salima, near the lake shore in central Malawi, the road runs below the escarpment on what could be the pre-historic shore line of Lake Nyasa, to Mangochi, down toward the southernmost tip of the Lake.

If you trundle down this rather well maintained road you will suddenly be confronted with taller than life size figures of dancing warriors, feathered head-dresses and hide kilts frozen in a swirl of movement, each dancer carved entirely from a single piece of wood. Rotund face masks, almost a metre across, smile benignly from coronas of carved feathers, the pale wood buffed to a rich glow. After seeing millions of little tourist trinkets, these are almost breath-stopping.

They are certainly car-stopping. We screeched to a halt, and discovered that the artists are among many trained at Mua Mission just a little way back up the road. The lure was irresistible. We turned back and branched off onto the dirt road to Mua parish.

The Catholic Mission Station is set above the road, perched between the steeply incised foothills and the flat wooded plain that sweeps to the lake. The first impression is of Victorian Catholic missions universally—red brick under terra cotta tiles, a double-storied central building with classic lines and Italianate arched cloisters, a sense of cleanliness, serenity and purpose. A hospital, a school, a church. A scamper of noisy children chasing a ball in the dusty road, dappled by the shade of the almost obligatory blue-gums.

The road ends in a small parking area, and we were led off to view the "display room". The path winds through an exuberant garden, half planned, half spontaneous, to a small rondavel under tall indigenous

trees. And for me the little building itself eclipsed the work inside.

Built in the traditional African mode of a conical thatched roof over a circle of hand-made bricks surrounded by a narrow open veranda, the single room structure is shaded by low eaves, supported by a palisade of wooden poles. These poles are in themselves an art exhibition. Each is patterned from base to roof, carved by hand into elegant chevrons and waves, basket-weave, candy twist and corduroy stripes, and each has a noble figure carved from the uppermost third—I didn't count them, but I suspect they are the apostles. Very kingly apostles, preoccupied and haughty, gazing woodenly out across the verdant garden and vibrant bougainvillaea to the tucked and pleated foot of the escarpment. They have their backs turned to the smooth curved shell of the little building, which has been another opportunity for artistic expression. Geometric shapes in clear earth colours are frescoed on the plaster, like African rhythms made visible.

The entire effect is so arresting that the contents of the show room was slow to draw me in. But once there, I was fascinated by the subject matter of the carvings. The expected Christian theme was almost swamped by traditional representations of spirits of the ancestors, masked dancers, totem animals, demons and deities. Scenes from daily life rub shoulders with the biblical, the holy family's flight from Egypt cheek by jowl with a wooden bas relief of village beer-brewing; a giant chameleon, Chechewa symbol of life, rolls a wooden eye at the Man of Sorrows nailed to a tree.

The work is intricate, detailed and varied. Unmistakably African in its unselfconscious primitivism, it is at times remarkably sophisticated. It has certainly reached heights that no curio-carver has ever aspired to before. The whole experience, the room, the carvings, the Mission, is remarkable.

We left two hours later, deep in thought, our minds full of images and our ears haunted by the distant sound of axes in the foothills.

Still Mua
8th November

Mua Mission and its Kungoni Art Craft Centre are well known in Malawi, yet few people seem to know of the impressive museum which is far more central to the Mission and its raison d'etre than the carvings.

Why has a mission station a museum, you may ask? Because of a French-Canadian priest called Father Claude Boucher, that's why. (And for South African readers, that's pronounced "bush-ay" and not like the cricket player. The Malawians call him Father Bushy)

Fr. Boucher came to Mua twenty years ago [7] and proceeded to break the mould of religious repression.

In the eyes of the young priest, the myth and mystery of the indigenous people's sacred rites followed a theme very close to Christianity. So he has made it his business to highlight the parallels. Instead of outlawing traditional forms of worship, he simply points out that we are all engaged in roughly the same thing. For example, from Fr. Boucher's point of view, ancestor worship is not such a foreign concept when you consider the communion of saints. "Enculturation", he calls it. He has so encouraged the absorption of local ritual into the Catholic liturgy that mass at Mua includes all the traditional musical instruments and regalia, and the essential dances.

All very easy to say in one paragraph, but obviously it's not something that can be achieved overnight. Before you can point out the parallels, you need to know the lore. And steadily Fr. Boucher set about learning all he could about the local culture.

Two decades later, he is probably one of the most knowledgeable people on the subject of Malawian culture. Certainly the most informed white person. His research resulted in a vast photographic record and a collection of traditional artefacts unequalled anywhere in southern Africa, possibly in the whole of Africa. Hence the museum.

It is housed in three huge rondavels, each highlighting an aspect of the work. The first contains

---

[7] At the time of writing

the church's involvement in central Africa generally, specifically the Catholic Church at Mua, which provided Africa with her first black Bishop.

From this, a door leads out and into the second circular hall, where the spiritual mythology of the cultures in Malawi is contained. It is overwhelming. The panoply of cultural spirits is each embodied in a mask. And these are genuine masks, not tourist gimmicks or careful replicas.

The room reminded me of a cross between a planetarium and a theatrical wardrobe. There is a sense of vastness, of multiplicity, of unfathomable and bewildering power idling in neutral. At the same time there is the suppressed excitement of incipient action, the feeling that at any second the door will burst open and intent people will stream in, step into these waiting personas, and the magic will begin. A powerful reminder that theatre has its roots in religion.

The third of the huge exhibition huts displays the historical background of each cultural group in Malawi, and shows their rites of passage: birth, initiation, marriage, death and burial—and their secret societies. I was suddenly aware that all the models displaying this treasure house of cultural finery are carved from wood. All the handiwork of Mua Mission's master craftsman. Staggering, yes. As my scientific adviser noted, the entire museum is an amazing blend of social scholarship and artistic design.

Perhaps the most impressive thing of all is that this huge amount of work, this extraordinary celebration of humanity and spiritual exploration, is the product of one man's vision and energy. He didn't just think about it. He actually did it. He started the carving school, the painting classes for the deaf and dumb; he personally studied the cultures and even became initiated into a secret society; he formulated the "enculturation" of the liturgy much to the initial disapproval of the Church; he designed and built the museum and mounted the displays.

And all this in his spare time, too. He mentioned that there are twenty-three churches under his care, and he has just two other priests to help him.

To add insult to injury he looks like a trim young Pavarotti. He met us in shorts, sandals and an embroidered African shirt, radiating good health despite the constant cigarette between his fingers. He obviously doesn't think that what he has done is extraordinary in any way. He is pleased with it, certainly, but not apparently aware of the magnitude of it. Guiding us through the museum his explanations showed his ongoing fascination for the cultures and his warm respect for the people.

Later we learned that there is the general understanding that Fr Boucher will not open his museum to the public. I'm told this is because most Malawians would not cope terribly well with the blatant exposition of their intensely private spiritual lives. Thought provoking.

Suddenly it's not surprising that Fr. Boucher is a controversial figure in Malawi. Not everyone is bowled over by the giant strides he has taken for the church. There is no consensus about the breakthrough in international understanding provided by his documentation and display of the cultures. For instance, another of the handful of white people ever admitted to a secret sect feels that Fr Boucher has done these cultures a singular disservice. Those masks are the reason. To the communities they are not masks, but the actual spirit itself. In buying them from impoverished groups, he has deprived that community of that particular spirit. A strong indictment indeed. Another form of religious repression?

Is it Newton's Law that mentions equal and opposite reactions? Is it impossible to achieve great good without doing great harm? It seems ironic that spreading the Good News is never without some bad news too.

Tsetse fly in the ointment
9th November

Greetings from muggy Malawi.

The last week has been not so much an overture to the full opera of the rains but a sort of sweltering orchestral warm-up, a vaguely discordant and experimental tuning. Clouds have rumbled up and then gone back to the change room as if they forgot something. Lilongwe's frogs are clearing their throats and swapping stories of the winter break in conversational vowel sounds: Ow oo ow? Aw ee. Ah ah ah! An occasional soloist toad burps a few bars in a tentative way.

About Wednesday we had a short shower, and it was wonderfully effective. Sluiced of dust, everything looked transformed; leaves electric green in the golden light of the setting sun and the rust brown fuzz of dried moss along the top of our garden wall gleaming a sudden chartreuse. It's brown again today despite the fact that there was a shower of notable proportions on Saturday, or so I'm told. The only proof I have of that is a sudden upsurge in our mosquito population.

We were away—engaged in unarmed combat with the mosquitoes in Liwonde National Park—for the weekend. It was a salutary experience for me, still relatively new to the excitement of camping and liable to view the occasional discomfort through the rose-tinted lens of novel adventure. Certainly it's a remarkable privilege to accompany the Advisor to Malawi's National Parks on his essential familiarisation trips to protected areas, and I've always thought of these outings as the epitome of delight. How clever, I thought, to achieve a job where people PAY you to do what is such fun!

Mmmm. Oh yes. Indeed.

In reality it goes a little like this: Race back from the office just before lunch. Hurl enough food for three days into the scoff-box and a couple of beers into the cooler, gather up the camping equipment and clobber, and stuff the lot into the 4x4. After five minutes of driving into the sticky mid-day heat, go back for the forgotten barbecue grid.

Once in the park, the last of the afternoon is taken up with meetings with the warden, the rangers and perhaps the extension officer. The longed-for ideal of setting up camp early enough to sit and enjoy the sunset doesn't happen. A likely clump of bush is usually selected as a campsite while the light fades, and the last touches of comfort—the table cloth, the folding chairs—are set out illuminated by a lead-light powered by the vehicle battery and strung from a convenient branch. Garish, but effective.

That's when the mosquitoes arrived this Friday. Within minutes we were the centre of an insectivorous feeding frenzy. Opening my mouth to voice a protest resulted in the discovery that mosquitoes have an unpleasantly bitter taste. We braved the onslaught for about 15 minutes and then fled, bedding precariously piled on the roof rack and loose chattels rattling in the cab. Not too bad a rout, though. The mattress only blew off once, and we found it again quite easily despite the absence of a moon.

Selecting a suitable camp-site in unfamiliar territory and in the dark is not easy. We headed away from the flood plain, around the rocky hill. If we got a bit higher we'd escape the mozzies and perhaps even pick up a slight breeze in the still night. That was the plan, anyway. Lurching over rocks and dry trampled clay beds on a long-forgotten track, we finally found a level place under tall marula trees, and set up camp for the second time.

Dawn after a restless night, and within a few minutes we knew it was a tsetse fly area, the horsefly-like bites providing a bit of early morning callisthenics.

And the marula trees were in full bloom. As the warmth grew, the scent of the blossoms drew in loud swarms of bees. Very thirsty bees. Attracted to any moisture. Like sweat, for instance. Suddenly smacking thoughtlessly at tsetse flies was not a possibility.

We were not attacked by bees since this was just innocent scavenging for moisture, but the number of them was frightening to me. They were as thick as the mosquitoes the night before. All this rampant insect life, and we haven't even got into the wet season yet! So, for the second time in about twelve hours, we struck camp with impressive swiftness.

This was the start of a normal working day for the Advisor, who turned up at his Local Advisory Council meeting looking slick, shiny and virtually creaseless.

I, on the other hand, looked utterly dishevelled, grime-rimmed and grouchy. I may indeed be privileged, and experience aspects of the protected wilderness that is not available to the average tourist, however any tourist would have been howling for a refund after a night like that. Roughing it is an adventure, and often the best adventures are only fun in retrospect. Even paradise had its serpent.

Of course it was still a pleasure, despite the discomfort. We took our mountain bikes along, and explored the bush pedalling sedately, hung about with binoculars and field-guides. Each minute section of mopane woodland seems so gracefully composed and balanced, as if arranged by an ikebana master. The birdlife is spectacular, and l saw four birds that are new to me; the collared palm thrush, the long-toed plover and the vivid enamelled beauty of Bohm's bee-eater and Lillian's lovebird.

So I'm not complaining, just pointing out that when I wax lyrical about experiences in wildlife areas, there is often a subtext that I chose to ignore.

Alice in Liwonde-land
15th November

It's remarkable how few people recognise the fantasy in science. For instance, who would have thought that there is any connection between the trail of a leguaan (or *Varanus niloticus*, the Nile monitor lizard) and the classical Greek wave-pattern design? Yet, for all we know the first may have inspired the second. Aah, you say, that is speculation, not science. True, but speculation based on observation, and what is science if not intelligent observation?

Walter Rose, in his book *Reptiles and Amphibians of Southern Africa*, says that the name leguaan stems from l'iguana, which makes perfect sense, both being rather large lizards. However, the iguana is mainly arboreal and vegetarian—the leguaan, both rock and water varieties, are mostly land-based and definitely carnivorous, like their larger relatives, the Komodo dragons. I remember being told that in Namibia's Etosha National Park, rock leguaans greatly outnumber lions, and can possibly be considered the more important predator.

Wandering (and wondering) through Malawi's Liwonde National Park, we stopped near Mvuu Lodge in a smooth sandy place to enjoy the scribblings left by the feet of a myriad passing denizens: the tiny little y-shaped prints of blue waxbills, the delicate divided heart-shaped impressions of impalas' hooves, the huge dog-like paw mark of a hyena. An ephemeral and artistic visitor's book.

Among these marks was a strong drawn line, embellished on either side by an intricate and almost symmetrical pattern of sweeping curlicues—the track of the water leguaan, its heavy dragging tail flanked by short hind-legs, with long toes trailing curved claws through the powdery sand.

The trail crossed the road and led to a low shrubby bush. We chose to follow back along the track and see where it had come from. It had been heading away from the dense riverine fringe, and as we pushed our way through the thicket our nostrils were assaulted by a fierce blend of ammonia and old fish.

Looking up into the branches ahead of us we could see almost two hundred white breasted cormorants roosting in a tree. As we moved we glimpsed more, and by the time we reached the colony, we realised there were possibly closer to a thousand of these sleek efficient fish feeders. Below them the bush was coated with layers of guano, every shrub and creeper plastered powdery white, the ground whitewashed. It was an almost lunar landscape, the strength of the nitrates having scalded the plants to death.

But it was certainly not a lifeless area. Above us the cormorants rose with a sound like golf umbrellas being shaken out, and around us the white pasted bushes shuddered with movement as leguaans scurried away. It must be a scavenger's paradise, if you can stand the smell. The white breasted cormorant breeds throughout the year, so there is a constant supply of eggs or young chicks for a wily lizard or two.

Glancing down, we saw the tracks of a Nile monitor across the whitened earth, the linear tail-drag mark, the—wait a minute—that tail's awfully big, even for a leguaan, and the feet-marks are not the same at all...

Just then I got the scientific opinion in my ear:

"Crocodile!" he murmured, "Look there!"

He pointed under a bush about two metres ahead of us, and there was the unmistakable mottled yellow-brown and green tail, complete with the raised vee of posterior scales that notch their way down the broad back.

"Must be about eight foot," Science muttered as he walked towards it with intense interest. I trailed nervously in his wake.

A metre from the croc we stopped and peered under the bush into a small malevolent eye. Lying sideways to us, the reptile was braced for a quick escape, its snout just a foot or two from the high river-bank. It looked so solid and invincible that it's hard to imagine that its nervousness probably matched my own.

The croc shuffled forward a few rapid steps, then opened its startlingly long mouth and growled at us! A remarkable sound, a vast hissing like a punctured tractor tyre followed swiftly by a hollow truncated roar, rather like the boom of an ostrich.

It wasn't waiting around to gauge the effect of its startling voice. As it roared it launched its ponderous bulk over the lip of the bank, and we heard it crash splashily into the river below.

We stood there, gawking at each other in amazement, both spattered with guano from the departing birds and surrounded by a reeking wasteland, feeling incredibly privileged to be there. Neither of us had ever heard a crocodile roar before—not surprising for me, but my advisor has been in the field for more than thirty years, and has never heard that sound.

This is what makes science, and natural science in particular, so like fantasy; you start off in one direction, pretty sure you know the outcome, and within minutes you find something utterly different, surprising or electrifying, and on occasions bizarre as much as fantastic.

Burgling beasties
17th November

Hello from the Warm wicked Heart of Africa.

In a world desensitised by media superlatives, a shock word has to be employed periodically to convey enthusiasm, like 'wicked' in place of the rather threadbare word 'wonderful'. I just want you to know I am not subscribing to fashionable verbiage here.

We got back from a visit to Lake Malawi National Park late last night—I'll be talking about the park itself and the enclave village of Chembe at Cape Maclear later—and although it wasn't our first visit to the Park, it was our first stay, and as always closer knowledge changed my initial impressions.

The area is a blend of natural beauty and human squalor and poses a number of difficult biodiversity questions. It also happens to be a World Heritage Site.

We sat beside the Environmental Education Centre in the Park on Sunday for an al fresco lunch, and got robbed by three baboons. It was so neatly co-ordinated and slickly executed, so filled with Chaplinesque slapstick, that it was hilarious. Two young baboons piled in through the open doors of the car to snatch mangoes off the back seat. We abandoned our table behind the car to evict them. The two of them, legs thrashing, arms flailing, utterly dead-pan, each chose to exit through opposite doors and collided in the middle in a thrashing tangle of tails and limbs, a creasingly funny comedy routine that would take hours of rehearsal and fine timing to look so spontaneous on film.

While we were folded double by these antics, a big dog baboon was carefully helping himself to fruit on our abandoned table—and took the rubbish bag too, just for good measure. He neatly caught our attention, allowing the two in the car to escape. It was all superbly timed. We lost three mangoes, a bunch of bananas and an apple. And had our rubbish thoroughly strewn around. However, it was a much more entertaining experience than when we were relieved of our luggage in Livingstone this time last year.

We got home late last night (Tuesday) and this morning our gardener, Henderson-of-the-big-grin, told us smilingly that our garden furniture went walk-about in our absence. But not to be distressed, since it had been located half-way to the airport.

Apparently the night-watchman woke Henderson at half-past one on Monday morning with the shame-faced admission that the table and chairs were gone. Henderson, having narrowly survived an armed-response to a false alarm last week, bravely pushed the panic button. Within minutes the grounds were crawling with Darth Vader lookalikes and huge hungry dogs. Needless to say Henderson didn't sleep for the rest of the night.

By eight that morning the security team was back. Could Henderson identify the furniture? He could. They took him to a road-side market on the airport road, and there was our missing garden stuff. The items are now in the custody of the police, together with one sniveller* who couldn't run as fast as his accomplices.

We digested this story with breakfast this morning. So much for my jaundiced view of the elaborate security precautions people take here—there are no less than three guard 'houses' on our hectare and a half—and the exterior of our home fair bristles with neon tubes. The entire perimeter wall is set with bulk-head lights half of which no longer function since when each bulb winks out I give a silent cheer—I dislike light-pollution as much as noise pollution.

However we have now been sternly warned by still-smiling Henderson, on behalf of the security team, to have the lights blazing when we're away, draw all the curtains, and shut all the windows. We feel quite sure that any half-way intelligent burglar would know at once that if all the windows are shut we couldn't possibly be inside.

It's not surprising that the stuff got swiped. It's utterly astounding that we'll get it back. Hooray for Henderson and the armed-with-dogs response guys.

To offset the good news the telephones are out of order, so getting online to post my newsletter is a problem. And next week there will be no news from me at all—I have to trudge back to South Africa to sort out a few things, driving there and back, and I'll be shuttling between pillar and post for ten days or so before getting back here.

Till we chat again, stay secure.

** This is a term supplied by my Scientific Advisor, who not only corrects my factual faults but also provides considerable quantities of creative verbiage. Wick-ked!!*

Reflections on "Alice"
22nd November

The really wonderful thing about our unexpected encounter with the crocodile in Malawi's Liwonde National Park centres on that heart-stopping growl.

This is pretty startling stuff. Crocodile and giraffe are the two animals that are thought to be utterly silent. I can understand about the giraffe.

God must have had such a job constructing that neck and all the special hydraulic equipment to stop the brain from bursting every time the giraffe lowers its head, that a minor item like a voice-box could easily have been overlooked. Especially in the rush to get everything done before the weekend. Besides, where would you put the Adam's apple in a giraffe? Up at the top where you can build up lots of voice pressure from that long tube of a throat, or down at the base end and use the tube as a resonator? Decisions, decisions!

Much the same applies to the croc. There is a rather elegant system of valves to shut the mouth area off from the breathing apparatus, so that old leviathan can hang onto his supper under water and not drown himself in the process. It makes a larynx site a bit of a problem. String the vocal chords across the throat where those unchewed chunks of flesh and whole flailing fish pass through, or in the breath passages—and have the terror of the inland waters utter effete nasal noises? Nah, forgeddit. With a face like that, who needs to say anything anyway?

Besides, it's too late to retro-fit a tongue, so articulation will be up to shit.

Actually the crocodile does have a couple of sounds that it makes. Hatchlings make a disarming little quacking twitter just before they break the leathery shell of the egg, which alerts mother croc to the fact that they are still buried under piles of sand. She sets about digging them out and carries them gently to the water in her mouth. It's a mothering instinct that is (I think) unique among reptiles.

The only other sound is made by males in the mating season. I've heard a recording of this sound. It's referred to as a roar, but it's not really that dignified. It sounds very much like Victorian plumbing—a sort of hollow rushing gurgle, reminiscent of emptying cisterns and echoing pipes. That sound is probably heard by the average wildlife park visitor about as often as they hear baby crocs hatching. Very, very seldom. Neither sound is easily identifiable in the bush, so even if you did hear them you might be mystified by the sound, but you would probably never guess you had caught a snatch of crocodile conversation.

Here's the thrill—we not only heard the croc, we actually saw it making that noise. And, as an added bonus, it was making that noise at us. This wasn't croc-to-croc communication, it was very clearly a cross-species comment. It was the seriously offensive sort of comment that I'd blush to repeat, but my Scientific Advisor assures me it was simply a defensive "I'm here, don't step on me". Hah! Scientists are so often suckered by logic!

Of course we've talked about this continually since it happened, and a number of interesting things have come up. For instance, we assumed the crocodile, and the leguaans which first attracted our attention, were there to scavenge eggs and chicks from the white-breasted cormorant colony. Yet we saw no nests. Not a single nest. Close to a thousand birds at an obviously permanent roost, and not a nest in sight. Very odd.

But if there were no nests, what were the lizards after? A leguaan will take eggs and hatchlings, even fledglings, but probably not a whole cormorant should one fortuitously drop off its perch. A croc would, but how often do cormorants turn up their toes in the roost? Probably not all that frequently; and not frequently enough to cause a croc to take up a regular post there. A post, moreover, that it was very reluctant to leave. The leguaans had no hesitation about hurling themselves into the long fall to the sanctuary of the water below. What was it that drew the croc up there, and kept it, so high above the level of the river?

We were there for such a short space of time, and it's unlikely that we will be able to get back again in the immediate future, so all we can do is speculate. Here's what I think: we know crocs dig their nests well above flood water level, often some distance from the river. We know the female hangs around after that, keeping an eye on things. We know that the biggest predator of crocodile eggs is the leguaan. So, putting all that together, I'd say we probably chased a female croc off her nest mound.

Makes perfect sense to me. When I suggested it to Science Himself, I was rewarded with a doubtful face and a sad half-shake of the head. I could see him thinking, "These incurably romantic journalists, always jumping to sensational conclusions. When will we ever get them to follow facts to a sensible conclusion?"

I'm content to leave him to his thoughts. For my money, we scared a mother crocodile off her nest. My story, and I'm sticking to it.

Lake Malawi National Park
29th November

The extraordinary thing about this World Heritage Site and the foremost of Malawi's National Parks is that nobody knows about it. Everyone (almost) knows all about Cape Maclear, and lots of people recognise the name Monkey Bay. But Lake Malawi National Park? Never heard of it. Even me—while writing it down, I find I want to put "St Lucia" after "Lake".

Does this make it a candidate for the 'best kept secret' tag? Um............ not really. The word secret implies that somebody would love to know. The overwhelming ethos at Lake Malawi National Park seems to be 'nobody cares'.

The fall of Malawi's topmost tourist attraction is a case of the ill wind. Back in the 'good' old days when South Africans were political skunks to the rest of the world, there was only one country in Africa ready to welcome these racist tourists. Malawi. Boere and boeresses visited in droves, since there was really nowhere else for them to go. Malawi, and Cape Maclear particularly, was the prime honeymoon or holiday destination in the 70s and 80s.

But the wind changed, and South Africans are welcome everywhere. Records kept by Golden Sands, the resort at Lake Malawi National Park, show tourist figures a tiny fraction of what they were about six years ago, when bad old South Africa became the new Rainbow Nation and had a whole lot of novel options for travel.

Looking at Golden Sands today, one can see the relics of what must have been heart-catchingly beautiful. The shattered terraces spill broken bricks down bald slopes; shards of concrete and rusting tins congregate in hollows, scattered with the fallen blossoms of flame trees and frangipani. The luxury bungalows have torn mosquito netting and limp curtains. Buckled paving catches at unwary feet. There is a sign in a patch of sand between brick-edged sand paths saying, "Please stay on the paths. If you walk on the grass you will kill it." The sign should have been replaced long ago with "We told you so." But the sand has been swept, and someone is taking an interest. Beside it, the Environmental Education Centre looks new and cared for.

Inside the impression fades. The aquarium is a depressing array of mostly empty tanks. Those that still hold water are so green with weed that nothing can be seen. A separate building houses the museum. Still interesting despite the dust and pillaging, it is in desperate need of refurbishment.

All of this overlooks a biscuit-coloured beach and the sparkling turquoise and teal of the crystal cool lake. Fragrant green flowers from the pod mahogany tree (*Afzelia quanzensis*) lay their waxy cheeks on the sand, and a thousand tiny fishes in the glassy shallows rush up to examine your toes. Across the water, forested and rocky islands look like heaped mohair blankets on biscuit bases, and the air is full of cormorants, kingfishers, fish eagles, wagtails, hamerkops and more.

In the heart of Lake Malawi National Park (the first freshwater conservation area in Africa) is Cape Maclear. It's a crescent of beach running from Otter Point to Chembe Lodge, and right in the middle of that is the enclave village of Chembe.

How do you run a National Park when smack in the middle of it is an area that is not classified as Park, and is home to an unknown number of people? Conservative estimates say five thousand people. Less optimistic are estimates of eight and ten thousand. All of them are supported by fishing, though the dusty relics of hand-hoed sandy fields between the village and the road show attempts at cultivation. This is the driest area of Malawi, and cultivation practices have not yet evolved to the use of animal-drawn ploughs, let alone irrigation. The turned sand sifts to the water's edge and incipient reed beds are showing the beginnings of a delta.

Mud-and-thatch houses with reed enclosed yards form a belt some ten to twelve houses deep along the line of the beach. It's an organic, erratic area of dwellings and fish-drying racks, tiny restaurants and the occasional tourist lodge, like Fat Monkeys, The Gap, Chembe Lodge and others.

There is a raffish charm and haunting picturesque quality to Chembe Village—commonly called Cape Maclear. If you like walking, want to get to know the good-natured locals, don't mind dust and can happily do without any luxuries, Cape

Maclear/Chembe Village is the place to be. Backpackers love it. The bulk of visitors seem to be under 25 years old.

Since access to the Village does not actually pass through an official gate, it's doubtful if visitors know they are surrounded by a National Park. Boating and snorkelling are popular, yet the fact that this area boasts the only under-water trail in Africa is unknown.

The first National Park in the world to protect tropical freshwater fish, of which there are over 600 species of the popular colourful aquarium-type cichlids; an internationally proclaimed World Heritage Site; the third largest rift valley lake in Africa; an intensely beautiful area of vitally important biodiversity—and it's all falling apart through plain grinding poverty.

However, the World Bank intends throwing money at the problem. It will be interesting to see if it makes any difference. Any volunteers to hold their breath?

December 1999

Malawi in the Silly Season
7th December

Another warm hello from the ditto heart of Africa.

I know I promised to write last week, but life got marginally out of hand. Even the story due up last Monday got lost in the post, electronically speaking. With any luck you will have been feeling deprived and will be twice as pleased to get my news.

The jaunt down south to sort out the intricacies of importing a battered old pick-up into Malawi was complicated by a mosquito.

For those of you who have not yet suffered the horror of a dose of malaria, please go and look up my "Funny Malarious" story. You'll find it quite amusing, but it points out that in reality malaria is no joke.

Ask my scientific adviser. He got it for the eighth time on the trip down south, and it gets progressively less entertaining each time. Compared to his two weeks in Harare wrestling the parasites, my 26 hour delay at the South African border (while the police upgraded their vehicle clearance computer system) was a total breeze. Still, here we are back safe and (thankfully) sound with a legal vehicle and nothing lost but time.

Much to my surprise, Malawi looks just about unchanged since our departure two weeks ago. I was sure the rains would make a dramatic difference. It's been atypically dry since we left, and the lush vivid green land is still to come. The sky is brassy and cloudless with a blustery wind—it feels like August.

Though the summer seems to have stalled, the Silly Season has rolled right on bringing with it that perennial remnant of colonialism, the Christmas Panto. I'm always fascinated by how the genetically reserved English throw themselves into startlingly exhibitionist lunacy in the form of amateur theatre, and the sillier the better.

I'm also intrigued by the choice of story-line. This year Lilongwe's Madsoc (the local Music And Drama SOCiety) chose "Babes in the Wood" as their pantomime title. That alone was interesting, since it's not an English fairy-tale. Was it Hans Christian Anderson, or the Brothers Grimm? I don't know, but it makes a change from boiled-beef-and-carrots-stories like Mother Goose, Puss-in-Boots, or Jack and the Bean Stalk.

As the play progressed it became increasingly clear that nobody knew much about the Babes in the Woods, but there was a great deal of general knowledge about Robin Hood. (So who says the woods weren't Sherwood Forest anyway?) The cast was respectably out-numbered by the audience, who at times were considerably noisier, but quantities of exuberant pleasure were extracted by both.

It's an interesting phenomenon, the annual expat pantomime, calling for not so much the suspension of disbelief as the suspension of all critical faculties. It is not for the faint-hearted, the pedantic or the perfectionist. In its raucous appreciation of foolishness and quiet, good-natured understanding of mishaps, the audience-cast relationship in a tropical pantomime is a microcosm of a community. You don't get that in cities these days. It may not be the latest Lloyd Webber road-show, but it's Malawi in a nutshell, and we loved it.

Try to stay sane in the commercial clutter of Christmas by remembering whose birthday it is—whose millennium for that matter.

Use it or lose it
13th December

This is the current battle-cry of international wildlife aid agencies in Africa. Mostly applied under the acronym CBNRM, community based natural resource management is the banner being carried through into the new millennium. Conservation is out, resource management is in.

Good thinking, chaps! Way to go! Wildlife isn't there for the aesthetic appreciation of the privileged few, it's there for the betterment of local mankind. And shame on him who suggests that natural resource management is just wildlife utilisation in a different guise! Hush your naughty mouth! Everyone knows that wildlife utilisation means ivory necklaces, fur coats and violence-centred champions of civilisation slaking their bloodlust with a bit of slaughter in the bush. Gross!

Resource management, on the other less sinister hand, means blameless actions such as harvesting thatching grass, collecting firewood and gathering a few oddments for medicinal purposes. All gentle things that wouldn't make even the greenest vegan uncomfortable.

Not true, as you will see, but I'm wandering off the point a bit. Let's get back to the fatal flaws in

CBNRM for Malawi. Firstly, let's look at population figures in The Warm Heart.

Back in 1987 it was estimated that there were ten million people in Malawi which, given the small size of the land, is a population density of 85 people per km^2. Most of these people are entirely dependent on the land for their livelihood—food production, energy, housing, all comes from biomass provided by that piece of ground. No wonder the land is looking a tad nibbled.

As far as health care is concerned, there is one Western doctor per 50 000 people, and roughly one traditional medical practitioner to every 140 people. It is unsurprising that most of the populous rely on traditional cures. It must also be remembered that traditional healers do more that cure physical ailments. They provide remedies for psychological and spiritual problems too. And the bulk of the treatments come from the wild.

There is a shrub that is helpful in predicting the future. The root and stem promote successful business. This is the cowpea, *Aeschynomene abyssinica*, and it's sold in very high volumes in Malawi. The plant itself is now so rare that it is imported from Mozambique. It would seem that in the case of this particular plant resource, management tactics are a little too late.

However, traditional treatments are not always plant material. A study undertaken by TRAFFIC (Trade Record Analysis of Fauna and Flora in Commerce) in east and southern Africa shows that about 185 animal species are used, ranging from lion skin for courage, or the dung of a kingfisher for eye problems, to an entire grasshopper to regulate a rapid heart rate. It's hardly a problem when it comes to gobbling a grasshopper or harvesting a dab of kingfisher poo, but obtaining a lion skin calls for a fair amount of sacrifice on the part of the lion. If you can find one.

One of the most desirable creatures from a traditional healing point of view is the pangolin (*Manis temminckii*), an endearing animal that looks like a huge ambulatory pine-cone. Sheathed almost from nose to tail tip with large overlapping horny scales, pangolins are solitary and naturally scarce. Being ant and termite eaters, they are nocturnal in the hot summer months, often crepuscular and can occasionally be seen during the day in winter. But let me tell you, you are very, very, very fortunate to see one at all. I've been prowling through the bush for years, and I have yet to spot one.

It's the pangolin's protective scales that make it valuable to traditional medical practitioners throughout south and eastern Africa. These cure nosebleeds, rheumatism, provide good luck, are essential in rain-making rituals, and are good for warding off lions and other wild animals, not to mention providing protection against bad omens. If that's not enough, they are also used to treat heart problems, are proof against bullets, help to position the foetus in pregnancy and expel the placenta after. They are also good for unspecified psycho-social ills and as a love charm. And they can be used in the treatment of cattle—and make efficient spoons.

(Before you suck in your breath at the appalling gullibility of the poor rural masses, just remember that the South American nine-banded armadillo is being used in the search for a cure for leprosy, and that early man was curing headaches by chewing willow bark—a natural source of aspirin.)

How many pangolins do you think Malawi still has? Would you imagine this to be a resource that can be used sustainably by the community?

These are just two examples of a very real problem. It's a bit pointless telling people that sharing resources will make them better off when the resources have long since been used to the brink of extinction. You can't invite people in to dinner when the fridge is empty.

In our childhood we were told about Old Mother Hubbard and her bare cupboard problem, but we were not told about the poor doggie's sense of disappointment and failed expectations. I wonder if the impoverished rural communities in Malawi who are being subjected to the CBNRM efforts of international aid givers will be as reticent.

Lilongwe for the birds
13th December

Season's greetings from the Warm Heart.

It's been an exciting week on the bird front in our little patch of Africa. All the trees in our garden are now in full leaf, which makes it a tad cooler and prettier, but cuts down a little on the visibility of the birds. All the same this week has brought two new sightings for me, and the identification of my problem bird.

I've been muttering about this last ever since we arrived in August. The call has been taunting us for five months, and I'd asked around, but it's hard to mimic a call when you mouth is furnished with lips and teeth. I named it 'the squeaky wheel bird' which was clearly misleading, since I got suggestions ranging from the olive sun bird to the pearl-spotted owlet. Perhaps it would have been better, if clumsier, to say that the call is more like brakes being applied to a spinning wheel. It starts high and fast, and falls in tone and pace five or six times each call.

I thought I'd spotted the blighter in Liwonde National Park, but the bird I saw turned out to be a tchagra. I felt so silly. I couldn't understand how I made such a mistake. But when we listened to the bird call tapes I brought back from South Africa, there it was—the unmistakable falling and slowing call, identified as the three-streaked tchagra. Oh sweet vindication! It's the black-crowned that has the melodious song I know so well, silly me to confuse them. And the threestreaked—called simply the brown-headed here in Malawi—gives the wheel-slowing-call during aerial display, so while we were looking into the branches to spot him, he was circling way above the trees. Then he drops almost to the ground, and we'd be looking too high. But we've got him at last!

The second thrill was to see what the Afrikaners call the 'striped new-year's bird'. We spotted him (or her) as a big cuckoo shape way up in a combretum. It sat quite serenely while we dodged about with binoculars getting a really good squizz at it. Much muttering and turning of field guide pages later, we discovered him to be the striped cuckoo—a large and handsome fellow, black and crested, with snowy breast streaked with black at throat and thighs. As always there is a special sense of privilege spotting a bird for the first time. The southern African bird equivalent of the Oxford Dictionary gives the striped cuckoo's hosts as babblers and perhaps lesser masked weaver. Looking at the sheer size of the bird it's hard to picture it squeezing into any weaver's nest at all. Nice of him to pitch up almost on cue and justify the vernacular name from down south.

The third bird incident this week was both thrilling and heart wrenching. Looking up from breakfast on the veranda yesterday I saw a hunched grey form in my birdbath. While the cereal got soggy we pussy-footed to the bedroom window to get a look at the visitors face.

Above the softly barred breast, the noble head of a hawk gazed blindly forward, ruby eyes half closed. A little banded goshawk—but ill, very ill. Immobile feet braced in the cooling water, body supported by tail and wingtips, the small raptor was oblivious to anything.

Throughout breakfast we debated the matter. Should we leave him in peace to recover or die undisturbed? Or should we rush him to a vet in the hopes of effecting a cure, but unavoidably cause the suffering bird huge stress? Would the shock of capture kill him anyway? But if death was inevitable, would soon and sudden be preferable to later and lingering?

When he staggered for the second time I couldn't stand it. The bird barely flinched when my scientific advisor gently picked him up, and the strong weaponed feet made no attempt to grasp, though the cherry-red eyes opened fully for the first time.

The trip was pointless. The little dove-grey body gave up within minutes, probably the result of secondary poisoning caused by eating a poisoned mouse or rat. We brought back the sad and stiffening bundle and buried him—or her—beneath a velvet bush willow in the garden.

We lead such a cushioned existence so far from the full cycle of life, the blood of birth, the grey agony of death. We've forgotten how the two are linked as the covers of a book. I grieved for the little banded goshawk, but guiltily, wondering if I would be half as moved by the death of one of the numerous doves or bulbuls. Why should one bird's passing be worse than another, simply because I'd never seen it before?

Passing is part of life—without a close there can be no new start; seeds die to produce the new plants. The old year gives way to the new. Sober thoughts for Advent, entirely in keeping.

Christmas Bunny
20ᵗʰ December

Is Brer Rabbit still around? The good-natured, wily hero of North American folk tales, Brer Rabbit is not American by birth. He was captured along with central African slaves, and Afro-American Uncle Remus helped him to find his way into the hearts of children around the world. Malawi, like most African countries, has a rich oral tradition and among the host of heroes is Kalula the Rabbit, almost certainly the ancestor of Brer Rabbit. Perhaps today we would spell it Bra Rabbit. This is a Malawian story that features two of Kalula's friends, the bushbaby (*Galago moholi*) and the elephant shrew (*Petrodomus tetradactylus*)

Long, long ago Changa the Bushbaby and Nsulu the Shrew fell in love with the distant rosy twinkling of a veld fire. It was so very pretty, a dancing necklace of fiery beads on the throat of the mountain. How nice it would be to own a fragment of that distant beauty, to keep a spark and watch it dance whenever they pleased.

As they stood gazing at the far creeping line of flames, Kalula the Rabbit came past and asked why they looked so wistful. They told him about their longing to have their own fire, and Kalula the Rabbit, being wise beyond his stature, suggested they could find an ember where people were. In fact, if he remembered correctly, there used to be a village just two days' march away.

So Changa the Bushbaby and Nsulu the Shrew set off together. Now two days' march is not very far, but when your legs are very short and your feet very small, the distance is almost doubled. For the two little friends, it was a very tiring journey.

At last they reached the village, and their hearts sank. The people had moved on, and all the cooking fires were long since dead. They poked at the cold grey ashes despondently.

Just then Nkoswe the Rat popped up, and told them the villagers had moved to a fresher piece of farming land just two days' march away, and he, Nkoswe the Rat, could point out the direction.

The tired friends looked at each other. Two days' march! And each with four tiny, very tired feet. But they had come so far, and with such hope, it seemed silly to give up now. So once again they set off.

A few hours later Changa the Bushbaby gave a little squeal and sat down sucking his paw. Gently Nsulu the Shrew took the little leathery foot in his own tiny claws and examined it. A nasty thorn had broken off deep in the centre pad. Poor Changa. Walking on that paw was out of the question, and they had such a long way still to go.

So Changa the Bushbaby rested in a tree where he could watch the path, and Nsulu the Shrew bounded off as fast as his little legs could carry him to find an ember of fire.

At last Nsulu the Shrew reached the settlement and, quickly scooping a live coal onto a potshard, he turned right around and set off the way he had come. As he went he blew on the ember to keep it glowing. He scampered and hopped and blew, and blew and hopped and scampered until his face and his feet ached, but he didn't stop once for a day and a half until he came to the tree where Changa the Bushbaby waited.

Meanwhile, Changa the Bushbaby has spent all the time since his friend left with his eyes fixed on the path. He waited and he watched and licked his sore paw and watched and waited. When night fell he didn't dare sleep. What if Nsulu the Shrew came past in the dark, and Changa the Bushbaby missed him? So he stretched his eyes wide and watched all the harder. He watched and waited till his eyes smarted, but he didn't close them once until he saw Nsulu the Shrew bobbing down the path towards him, his eyes shining like the glowing rosy coal he held out before him.

Once the friends disentangled themselves from their first hearty greeting, and drew back to look at each other as long parted friends do, they were both astounded. Nsulu the Shrew's mouth has stretched forward into a long whiffley muzzle with the constant blowing, and Changa the Bushbaby's eyes had stretched to twice their size with the constant staring—and they have stayed that way to this very day.

The moral, I suppose, is that dedication to achieving a supremely difficult task will develop strong personal characteristics—but for me it says quite plainly that whoever searches for and finds The Light will fundamentally change forever.

Merry Christmas
21ˢᵗ December

Heartfelt hello from Way Down South

It's a strange sensation to step out of the bush into the whirling vortex of Yuppiedom. Plettenburg Bay, for seven months of the year, is a slow and pretty town perched on high ground above the Indian Ocean, its tree-graced, vine-hung slopes terminating in serene blue sea. Waves dash their lace petticoats against grey boulders on the shore and sandpipers chase the retreating tide over slow sweeps of gold and gleaming sand. At midyear whales come to calve in the bay, watched by the inhabitants with gentle awe, and by the visitors with extreme excitement.

In December Plett becomes a suburb of Johannesburg. As they do at Easter and in July, the commercial capital's townies forsake the inland street cafes and shopping malls and clog the seaside town with German cars and American fashions, everyone anxious to do some exotic shopping.

For once I sympathise. Lilongwe is a delight, but it doesn't profess to be a Mecca for the spendiferous. I feel quite besotted with the bustle, the book shops, the fashion stores... frozen tofu! ... fat-free anything at all! ... more than three styles of shoe! .... The delights are almost endless. Almost. People-poisoning tends to limit my range a bit, and returning to the serenity of the family protea farm is bliss.

South Africa's southern Cape has an even climate with little variation between summer and winter and modest rain all year round, but wet weather peaks at the change of seasons. This year it's drier than ever before, though neither the proteas nor the tourists are complaining. I arrived in thin drizzle and thought I'd brought the wet with me, but the skies have cleared again and I hope the rain is getting into its stride in Lilongwe.

The rains were just beginning as we left. Voluptuous clouds build through the bright mornings and gentle soothing rain sifts through the afternoons into the night. Once it stops the insect sounds are as all-pervasive as the sound of drizzle, and the frogs are unusually silent. We think we've found out why.

After a shower one evening, working with the doors open to encourage a feeble breeze to come indoors, a cloud of flying ants took the invitation and invaded *en mass*. Following them came a small but enthusiastic frog. I watched as this diminutive creature demolished every flying ant it could spy, stopping after each four-swallow-ant to do a slow and sensuous shimmy to compact the contents of its bulging belly. We think the frogs don't sing after the rain because, just then, their mouths are full. No doubt most of us will feel equally in need of a

slow shimmy after the traditional engorgement of Christmas dinner.

No letter from me next week, I hope to be exploring distant parts of Zimbabwe, if the country's dearth of diesel fuel allows! I'll tell you all about it when I return to Lilongwe around the 10th of January.

So, till then, all good wishes for a most blessed Christmas and a fun-filled New Year.

Full Circle
27th December

The door to the next millennium stands ajar and it's almost impossible not to glance back before rushing through. It's been a busy century, let alone millennium! As far as conservation is concerned not much happened in the first thousand years—there wasn't much need to conserve anything, we were too busy just staying alive.

Back then the people were few and the resources many. Slash and burn agriculture was a perfect strategy, since the same patch of land would rest perhaps for 150 years before being cultivated again. When mankind was not staying out of the way of wildlife he was sneakily snitching the odd meal from a leopard or a cheetah, or working out how to kill things to eat without any personal danger, like pits, arrows and snares. It was a hand-to-mouth, hard life. Infant mortality was huge, and anyone who made it past puberty would probably pop off before forty anyway.

By the last century man had come to terms with his environment. They were a victor's terms. Anything that didn't actually contribute to the obvious and immediate good of the 'civilised' world was expendable—or fiddled with until a use was found for it.

Animals that were not of any obvious use were admired for their strangeness and beauty, and for their extravagant abundance. Man's distance killing skills had advanced considerably, and a few thousand moving targets was just too much to resist. The 19th century saw the wholesale destruction of wildlife on an unprecedented scale.

By the 20th century, whenever Western man stopped fighting himself long enough to look around, he could see the scales tipping. Humans were thriving and wildlife was thinning. The first areas of land were 'reserved' for wildlife only and hunting in them was forbidden.

Three quarters of the way through the century, more children were surviving infancy and more adults staying alive past 60 than ever before, and the world got very small indeed. True wilderness had almost vanished. More people were evicted from more land to make more wildlife sanctuaries.

And here we are on the doorstep of the second thousand years, looking back and saying, "Actually the people on the land were doing all the right things back then, before Western interference. So let's bring them into the reserves again and help them to remember the old management techniques they used back two centuries ago. We'll call it CBNRM."

In some cases it's too late. The scale has tipped too far, mankind is too many and the resources too few. There are Community Based Natural Resource Management efforts that were successful, like some of the Zimbabwean Campfire projects. But in areas where humanity dominates the biomass, there are simply not enough resources to go around comfortably and have enough left for tomorrow.

The realization must be made that, though the wheel has come full circle, we are considerably further down the road than before and the scenery has changed. The challenge for the 21st century and the 2nd millennium is to find a way to redress the imbalance.

To me it seems that Mother Nature is working on the problem by a resurgence of diseases we thought we had licked in the 50s, like malaria and TB, and a few new ideas of her own like AIDs.

My wish for the new century is that we spend as much time and money on solving conservation and environmental problems as we do on health issues. What's the point of preserving human life if our contact with wilderness is reduced to encounters with cockroaches and the few weeds that push their way through the cracks in concrete?

And for the millennium? That's too big to wish for, it's like making plans for the sun.

About the Author

For more than a decade Sandy Dacombe produced and presented the popular radio programme Talking of Nature on the national English radio station, Radio South Africa. This not only provided more fun than is decent to contemplate, but it also gained her two journalism awards for conservation and environmental awareness.

Trained for the stage, Sandy amassed a wealth of experience in just about everything else, from selling biscuits to designing 'haute clobber', from teaching speech and drama to running an art gallery, from radio plays to patchwork quilts, from floristry to newsletters, from public speaking to editing, from television scripts to backyard blogging.

Apart from her passion for wildlife, Sandy is equally enthusiastic about travel. She has swum with the dolphins of Australia's Monkey Mia, been bewitched by the rock-paintings of Tsodilo Hills in Botswana, had her heart wrung by the elegance of moonlit doum palms in northern Kenya's Samburu, and stood frozen—almost eyeball to eyeball—with a leopard at En Gedi above the Dead Sea.

In her twenties a motor accident put her in hospital for almost a year, an experience which forced her to (literally) stand on her own feet as she learned to walk again. The loss of almost half of her right foot meant a much greater gain in personal determination and plain cussedness. To her mind it's been a reasonable bargain.

Since the reliance has had to be more on the cerebral and verbal than the physical for much of her life, Sandy has gained considerable skill in manipulating language, and though once described as a jargonnaut, she prefers the wider implications of the title Wordsmith. Self-employed as copy editor, author, script writer and voice-over artist, she is a natural communicator with an infectious love of life, and the kind of laugh that you either love or loathe. Luckily, as a reader you won't have to make that choice.

Science—a sort of explanation

Anyone who spends time writing up matters related to science, no matter how casually, needs to develop a rapport with a scientist involved in that branch or wing or discipline or whatever it is called scientifically. I found this especially so while engaged in radio work. Since I was being paid to be responsible about what was fed to the gullible public, I needed an approachable, knowledgeable, media-wise advisor who could scan the work for possible submarines, and yet take the embellishments of fact as mere dramatic flair, and not as wilful deviations from the truth as many scientists do.

I have been most fortunate in discovering several such paragons. Vincent Carruthers, Dr Alan

Kemp, Dr Mike Bingham and Dr John Wilson are among them, and I remain indebted to them. But head and shoulders above the above-average, was a man blessed with a beautiful speaking voice, an instinctive understanding of the theatre inherent in communication, and a wide ranging enthusiasm for, and understanding of, nature in all its complexities. He has infinite patience coupled with a forthright manner, and a wonderful sense of humour. This man is Tony Ferrar.

Antony Auriol Ferrar was born, the second son in a family of four children, to a military father and actress mother who left an exhausted England after the Second World War. They set about farming among the granite-boulder outcrops of a young Rhodesia, and the landscape filled the hearts and souls of the children as only a wild, free landscape can.

Tony studied animal husbandry and agriculture at South Africa's University of Natal, Pietermaritzburg. Then came a moment, while on holiday in the Zambezi valley, when he sat in a tree and had an elephant pass right underneath him. Had he simply stretched out with his toe he could have touched its back. Once it was gone, he climbed down and stood where it had stood. The soft mown-grass scent of elephants filled his nostrils, and he fell in love. He applied for a post in the Zimbabwe Wildlife Department and was accepted, and while with them did his Master's Degree in Wildlife Ecology at the University of Harare.

Since then his life has been almost evenly shared between the academic, the administrative, the advisory and the adventurous. In his 50th year he "switched from eco-missionary to eco-mercenary" giving up his last formal job—as CEO of the Wildlife and Environment Society in South Africa—for the uncertain benefits of life as a freelance consultant.

He has worked in a wildlife and tourism advisory and/or park planning capacity in Zimbabwe, South Africa, Botswana, Namibia, Zambia and Malawi, and Guatemala.

This is my Scientific Advisor, more commonly called Science in my writing. There are times when I think he ought to be sainted, but perhaps the world would be better off if he were cloned.

Acknowledgments

Thank you to everyone who enjoyed my stories and letters on the web and asked for them to be published in book form. Your enthusiasm has been a motivating force.

More specifically, thanks to Shelagh Nation for her diligent editing and sage advice; without your help this book may have been longer, but would be much less than it is. Besides, without your guidance, Shelagh, I would have had nothing to write about.

Profound thanks to my mother Shirley Isaac and my brother Hugh who printed out every blog and newsletter I wrote for the web, and kept them. I never thought to do so. The original web site is no more, and without their private stash, my writing would have proved as ephemeral as a radio broadcast.

Thanks also to the late Dr Andrew McKenzie who encouraged me to begin the XAfrica series for WildnetAfrica, and to Frank Johnston of Central Africana Ltd in Malawi, who thought highly enough of my web-words (edited to a professional, impersonal, narrative) to publish with his exquisite photographs in *Malawi, the warm heart of Africa* in 2002.

Leigh Brandt and Stephen Allen in Barberton rescued me from drowing in the problem of designing my own book, thank you both for much needed assistance.

As an arts trained person, I could never have imagined that Science would loom so large in my life. I would be lost without him.

Soli Deo Gloria

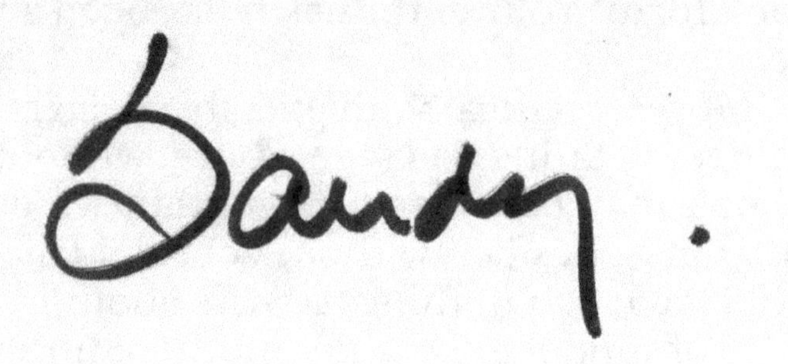

www.ingramcontent.com/pod-product-compliance
Lightning Source LLC
Chambersburg PA
CBHW050908260726
48660CB00001B/97